creative
WORKSHOP

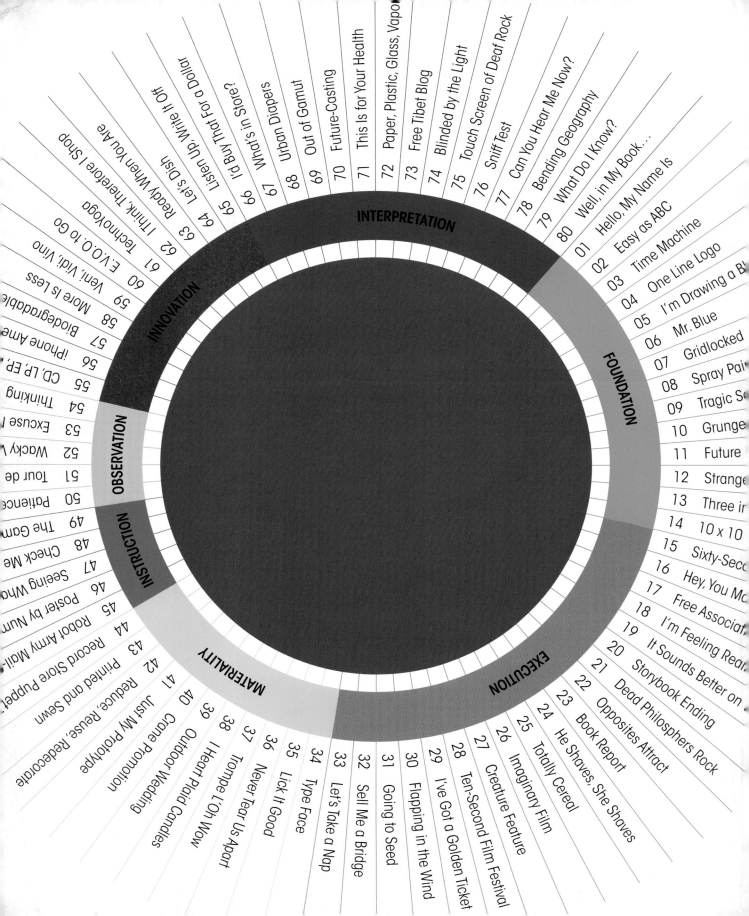

INTERPRETATION

INNOVATION

OBSERVATION

INSTRUCTION

MATERIALITY

EXECUTION

FOUNDATION

71 This Is for Your Health
72 Paper, Plastic, Glass, Vapo...
73 Free Tibet Blog
74 Blinded by the Light
75 Touch Screen of Deaf Rock
76 Sniff Test
77 Can You Hear Me Now?
78 Bending Geography
79 What Do I Know?
80 Well, in My Book...
01 Hello, My Name Is
02 Easy as ABC
03 Time Machine
04 One Line Logo
05 I'm Drawing a B...
06 Mr. Blue
07 Gridlocked
08 Spray Pai...
09 Tragic S...
10 Grunge
11 Future
12 Strange
13 Three i...
14 10 x 10
15 Sixty-Seco...
16 Hey, You Ma...
17 Free Associat...
18 I'm Feeling Rea...
19 It Sounds Better on...
20 Storybook Ending
21 Dead Philosphers Rock
22 Opposites Attract
23 Book Report
24 He Shaves, She Shaves
25 Totally Cereal
26 Imaginary Film
27 Creature Feature
28 Ten-Second Film Festival
29 I've Got a Golden Ticket
30 Flapping in the Wind
31 Going to Seed
32 Sell Me a Bridge
33 Let's Take a Nap
34 Type Face
35 Lick It Good
36 Never Tear Us Apart
37 Trompe L'Oh Wow
38 I Heart Plaid Candles
39 Outdoor Wedding
40 Crane Promotion
41 Just My Prototype
42 Reduce, Reuse, Redecorate
43 Printed and Sewn
44 Record Store Puppet...
45 Robot Army Mail...
46 Poster by Num...
47 Seeing Wha...
48 Check Me...
49 The Gam...
50 Patience...
51 Tour de...
52 Wacky V...
53 Excuse ...
54 Thinking...
55 CD, LP, EP...
56 iPhone Ame...
57 Biodegradable
58 More Is Less
59 Veni, Vidi, Vino
60 E.V.O.O. to Go
61 Technoyoga
62 I Think, Therefore I Shop
63 Ready When You Are
64 Let's Dish
65 Listen Up, Write It Off
66 I'd Buy That For a Dollar
67 What's in Store?
68 Urban Diapers
69 Out of Gamut
70 Future-Casting

creative
WORKSHOP

80 challenges to sharpen your design skills

DAVID SHERWIN

HOW
BOOKS

Cincinnati, Ohio
www.howdesign.com

For more excellent books and resources for designers, visit www.howdesign.com.

14 13 12   5 4 3

Distributed in Canada by Fraser Direct
100 Armstrong Avenue
Georgetown, Ontario, Canada L7G 5S4
Tel: (905) 877-4411

Distributed in the U.K and Europe
by F+W Media International
Brunel House, Newton Abbot, Devon, TQ12 4PU, England
Tel: (+44) 1626-323200, Fax: (+44) 1626-323319
E-mail: postmaster@davidandcharles.co.uk

Distributed in Australia by Capricorn Link
P.O. Box 704, Windsor, NSW 2756 Australia
Tel: (02) 4577-3555

Library of Congress Cataloging-in-Publication Data

Sherwin, David.
  Creative workshop / David Sherwin.
      p. cm.
   ISBN 978-1-60061-797-3 (pbk. : alk. paper)
  1. Creative ability--Problems, exercises, etc. I. Title.
  BF408.S4486 2010
  153.3'5--dc22
                              2010022826

Edited by **AMY SCHELL OWEN**
Designed by **GRACE RING**
Production coordinated by **GREG NOCK**

ABOUT THE AUTHOR

© Mary Paynter Sherwin

David Sherwin is an award-winning designer and art director with a depth of expertise in developing compelling creative solutions for challenging business problems.

He has worked at a wide range of creative agencies, from large marketing consultancies to smaller interactive agencies. His clients have included AT&T, Cingular Wireless, Holland America Line, Onyx, Microsoft, Toshiba, T-Mobile and many others.

He is currently Senior Interaction Designer at frog design, a global innovation firm, where he helps to guide the research, strategy and design of novel products and services for some of today's leading companies.

David is an active speaker and teacher, and his writing has appeared in A List Apart, design mind and other periodicals. He currently lives in Seattle with his wife, the poet Mary Paynter Sherwin. In his free time, he maintains the blog ChangeOrder: Business + Process of Design at http://changeorderblog.com.

CONTENTS

Introduction

"Difficult situations breed astonishing results."
— Jeffrey Veen

Have you ever struggled to complete a design project on time? Or felt that having a tight deadline stifled your capacity for maximum creativity? This book is for you.

Within these pages, you'll find eighty creative challenges to help you reach a breadth of innovative design solutions, in various media, within any set time period. By completing these challenges, you'll round out your skills by exploring projects along the full continuum of design disciplines, from the bread and butter of branding and collateral to the wild world of advertising to the user-centered practices of creating interactive projects. Along the way, we'll take brief forays into wayfinding, editorial design, video and motion graphics, and many other areas of our continually expanding practice.

To aid you in conquering these challenges, I'll provide useful brainstorming techniques and strategies for success. By road-testing these techniques as you attempt each challenge, you'll find new and more effective ways of solving tough design problems and bringing your solutions to life.

BECOMING MORE CREATIVE TAKES PRACTICE

Designers are often encouraged to bluff their way through unfamiliar deliverables in order to bootstrap their way toward a stable career, and my experience was no different. My first decade as a designer was humbling. A typical day in the life looked like this:

Two fresh logo sketches for your new wine bar by tomorrow? Catalog cover designs for your cruise line's venture into South America? Home and secondary page user interface examples for a technology consulting web site by Friday? No problem. I'll figure things out before I collapse on my keyboard, exhausted, at 2:00 A.M.

During those years in the trenches, I discovered that:

Failure is a necessary component of creativity.

Well-seasoned designers understand that resilience in the face of repeated failure is the only path to success. Improving as a designer requires us to consciously choose to explore novel territory as part of our daily work. David Kelley from IDEO calls this "enlightened trial and error," and it is the best way to seek out a great result that fulfills your client's business need.

Process is more important than the final product.

As architect Matthew Frederick notes, "Being process-oriented, not product-driven, is the most important and difficult skill for a designer to develop." Being aware of your working process as a designer and reshaping it to fit the problem presented to you is a lifelong practice that will define your career. However, don't forget what Mark Rolston of frog design says:

Topics Covered in This Book

Trying these eighty challenges will take you on a trip through most of today's prominent design disciplines. They're organized into the following categories:

FOUNDATION SKILLS
- copywriting
- design history
- grid systems
- illustration
- paper engineering
- photography
- physical prototyping
- research
- typography

WORK DISCIPLINES

Advertising and Marketing
- guerrilla tactics
- online ads
- out of home ads
- print ads
- posters
- TV commercials

Branding
- annual reports
- collateral

- identity development
- product packaging

Editorial and Film
- book covers
- magazine layout
- music packaging
- film posters

Interactive Media
- information architecture
- interaction storyboarding
- user interface design

Product Design

Store Design and Wayfinding
- environmental graphics
- retail store experiences
- trade show booths
- wayfinding

Type Design

Video and Motion Graphics
- hand animation
- storyboarding

"Plans are no substitute for the real thing… Process is a means to an end. Our purpose is to create."

Rote repetition rarely leads to deep design intuition.

Your design process consists of the living, breathing flow of actions that you take—some conscious, some unconscious—as part of solving a client problem. As you repeat similar types of design projects, you become more proficient in identifying which of these actions lead to a well-designed result. But we radically improve our skills when we are forced outside of our comfort zone and asked to solve problems that seem foreign, or use tools or methods that seem alien to us.

You'll never have enough time to work on a paid client project.

Having less time to work on a project can lead to more creative results, if you're smart about how you use that time. We often expend a good part of our projects bemoaning our lack of time to solve a client problem, rather than fully using our time to confront it. Deadlines come fast and furious, no matter whether you are a solo designer, work in-house at a company or have a role at a design firm or creative agency. Client deliverables will always verge outside your areas of expertise. A designer's career is more like a marathon than a series of sprints, and maintaining a productive, yet creative pace is the only way you'll stay sane.

Designers become more creative by learning to access their intuition.

We become better designers when our design skills are grounded in intuition. One of my favorite designers, Paul Rand, said, "The fundamental skill [of a designer] is talent. Talent is a rare commodity. It's all intuition. And you can't teach intuition." That's true. You can't teach intuition in a classroom lecture. But you can become more intuitive by solving wildly divergent design problems in a disciplined manner.

UNDER CONSTRAINTS, CREATIVITY THRIVES

Completing the eighty challenges in this book and abiding by the unique constraints of each design problem will force you to confront your inner critic and improve your working habits in order to keep the pace, as well as develop a clearer sense of how to access your design intuition in the pursuit of more meaningful design concepts and visual executions.

It will also teach you to embrace failure as part of your working process, and to become more confident in your capacity to create meaningful designs in any time frame.

These are worthwhile goals for anyone seeking a long-term career in design. Rather than being endlessly driven by the fear that you may not have enough talent to be the next über-designer of the century, you can be confident that you have the necessary skills to solve a greater breadth of design problems.

HOW TO COMPLETE A CHALLENGE

Getting Started

Before diving into solving a challenge, read it carefully. They've been crafted to test your design skills regarding everything from visual aesthetics to nuanced business strategy to product innovation. You may need to conduct research before you can complete the challenges in the last third of the book.

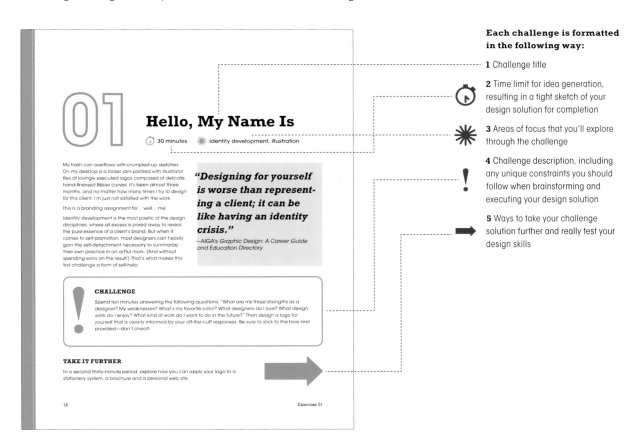

Each challenge is formatted in the following way:

1 Challenge title

2 Time limit for idea generation, resulting in a tight sketch of your design solution for completion

3 Areas of focus that you'll explore through the challenge

4 Challenge description, including any unique constraints you should follow when brainstorming and executing your design solution

5 Ways to take your challenge solution further and really test your design skills

What Tools Will You Use?

Here are some of the tools you can use when executing these creative challenges:

PRODUCTION TOOLS
- black marker
- colored markers and pencils
- colored paper
- craft knife
- cutting mat
- glue
- needle and thread
- pencils
- ruler
- tracing paper
- transparent tape

DIGITAL TOOLS
- digital camera or mobile device
- visual design software, such as
  Adobe Creative Suite

About the Time Limit

Each challenge includes a time limit for how long you can spend on idea generation. Within this time limit, you should be exploring a range of ideas with pencil sketches. Working with pencil and paper is the fastest way to land on a direction for a compelling design execution.

"Ask any great designer and they'll tell you they always doodle and generally start any design assignment by drawing," says design manager and strategist Daniel Schutzsmith. Creative director Carrie Byrne concurs: "By quickly sketching out ideas, the poor ones fade quickly from priority without wasting precious time executing them."

Moving From Sketch to Design Execution

After the time limit is up, gather the necessary tools and start executing the deliverables outlined in the challenge. Be sure to run your selected idea through the final litmus test: Is it meaningful? Experience designer, teacher and author Nathan Shedroff says

"Meaning is the most significant and powerful element of whatever people create for others." If your idea has deep meaning, it will encourage a more beautiful expression in the final design.

Should you jump into Adobe Illustrator, or reach for colored paper, scissors and glue? Based on what the challenge requires, your tools may vary. You can even explore mixing mediums or inventing a new way of executing your design idea. (Some of the challenges may require it!)

"Hybridize your tools in order to build unique things," says designer Bruce Mau. "Even simple tools that are your own can yield entirely new avenues of exploration. Remember, tools amplify our capacities, so even a small tool can make a big difference."

Know When to Move On

Don't become hung up on having a final, polished result for every challenge in this book. Your time is better spent attempting to solve all of the challenges with pencil and paper first.

This can be a real struggle if you're used to using a computer for your everyday design work. "There's something about sitting down and finessing an idea on the computer that can make it harder to let go of an idea that's just not working. Even when you know it's not!" says book designer Michel Vrana.

Whether you're executing the design for a business card or a complicated web site, your first stab at execution rarely feels complete. So, after you've undertaken your first attempt at realizing your idea via the appropriate medium, take a moment to evaluate if your concept holds up. If you aren't making progress, feel free to move on to another challenge.

DESIGNING FASTER BY TIMEBOXING

As you work on the creative challenges in this book, you'll end up throwing some of your accumulated knowledge about your design process out the window. No single designer can be an expert in all of these disciplines and types of projects—especially within the provided time limits. After completing a few dozen challenges, you may be forced into new ways of thinking about how to approach specific design activities. As a result, your process—from the way you approach a problem to how it is executed in layout—will evolve. In a sense, you'll start to design how you do design.

One of the ways you can definitely speed up your process is by using a time management technique called timeboxing. This technique is regularly used in the world of software development, but it's also useful for any creative professional looking to produce better work faster. The activity of timeboxing will teach you to switch on your creativity at will and to think more intuitively.

What Is Timeboxing?

In its simplest form, timeboxing is the use of short, structured sprints to achieve stated idea generation goals. That is, you use little boxes of time. When presented with a deadline, you take the first few minutes of the allotted time to plan out a series of manageable steps that have tangible work output, such as a set number of design ideas or sketches.

Why Should I Use Timeboxing?

Timeboxing is a great way to put structure around solving a design problem while avoiding the risk of aimless or unfocused idea generation. By stating your intent at the start of your process to solve a design problem, you can dismantle a thorny challenge into easily digestible nibbles. Working within a timebox forces you to focus and fill the time with your effort, which is great for days full of distractions. Any designer who struggles to meet deadlines can easily benefit from using this approach. The more you use timeboxing, the more effective you'll become as a creative thinker, and the less time you'll need to come up with a viable design idea.

How Do I Get Started?

Timeboxing requires you to plan the activities you'll be carrying out in each box, and that you step through them in the sequence you've prescribed. As an example, here's what it looked like when I solved Challenge 61, TechnoYoga:

Timeboxes for TechnoYoga / 120 minutes

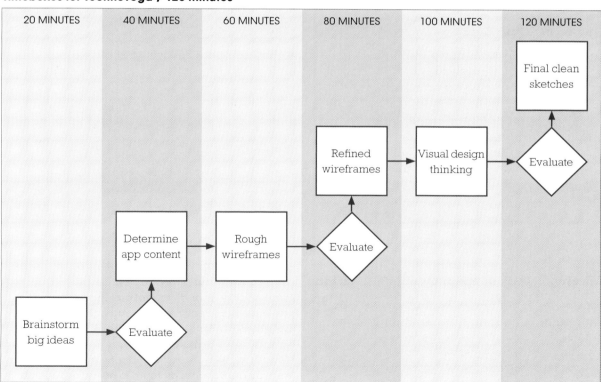

I recommend setting a timer with an alarm and training yourself to finish the deliverables in each timebox before the alarm goes off.

What Duration Should I Use for My Timeboxes?

Brief timeboxes are great for ideation and evaluation—ten to twenty minutes at most. As you attempt the challenges in this book, split the provided time limit into discrete activities and time them independently. The more time you give yourself, the less likely you'll be able to focus.

What Results Should I Expect?

Adopt this activity at your own pace. The first half-dozen times you try timeboxing, be realistic about the quality and quantity of output you can generate. Don't give up until you've given it a fair shake! It will take some practice for this activity to feel comfortable,

and there will always be occasions when you'll need to stop and work out details that couldn't be resolved in the time you had allotted.

USING BRAINSTORMING METHODS

Being Creative on a Deadline

> I've read through my first challenge. I'm ready to embark on my first twenty minutes of brainstorming. The timer is running. The blank page yawns before me like the arctic tundra...

Being creative on demand is, well, demanding. Sometimes the ideas won't flow without a little extra prodding of the brain cells.

If the idea of being creative under a deadline seems scary, use these brainstorming methods in your timeboxes as you solve the challenges in this book. They'll help you kick-start creative thoughts within a matter of minutes.

In brainstorming, everything in your mind is dumped on the page, much like emptying a drawer full of curiosities onto the floor. This yields clusters of words, pictures and ideas that suggest possible design directions. By avoiding formal logic and embracing impulse, all sorts of unusual ideas bubble to the surface. Once the notebook page is full, you can sift those elements to identify what may be of use.

Be sure to save the raw material from your brainstorms for potential use later. Often, these raw ideas end up informing your final designs and enhance the result.

Mind Mapping

This brainstorming method allows individuals or groups to identify a range of ideas quickly in a free-form manner.

1. In the center of your page, place the key point of focus for your brainstorm. It could be an insight or intuition that you gleaned from your research, a simple restatement of the problem or a potential direction for your solution.

2. Write words related to your key insight in the empty space around the center, radiating outward. If you run out of concepts, write down related things, opposites or thoughts that may seem unrelated.

Ideate, Evaluate, Iterate

Build time into your idea generation process to evaluate your design sketches. Don't fall in love with the first idea that seems to emerge magically from your mechanical pencil or Sharpie. Be willing to rethink your freshest ideas to see if there are any new, unexplored directions that will spawn even better ones.

The SCAMPER checklist is a time-tested tool that will help you. If you have a few strong ideas, putting them through this checklist will confirm their strength—and maybe even create some brand-new ideas.

Substitute something
Combine it with something else
Adapt something to it
Modify or **M**agnify it
Put it to some other use
Eliminate something
Reverse or **R**earrange it

This idea synthesis checklist was suggested by Alex Osborn, the advertising executive who coined the word "brainstorm." It was arranged into the SCAMPER mnemonic by writer Bob Eberle.

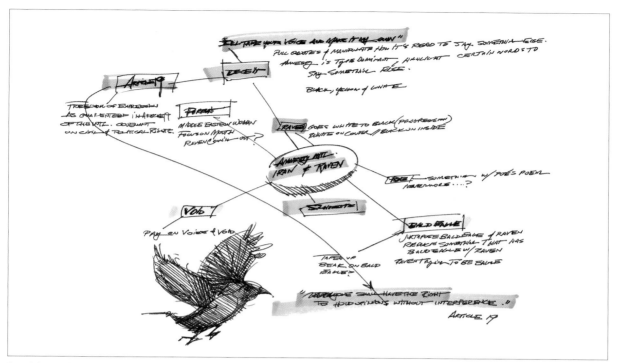

Sean Baker and Lenny Vella utilized mind mapping for the Free Association challenge. See page 53.

3. Expand upon relationships in the ideas that emerge from the various nodes; circle and group elements as necessary.

4. Distill big ideas from the map and run them through the SCAMPER checklist before starting to sketch out possible design executions.

Word Listing

This is an alternate method of mind mapping that has more structure and can yield quicker results.

1. On a sheet of paper, make three columns. In the first column, write as many concepts or terms as possible related to your point of focus for your design.

2. In the second column, pick an idea that interests you from the first column and write down a series of words related to it.

3. In the third column, write down words that are the opposite of the material you included in column one.

4. Circle and connect relationships that span columns one through three. Then, distill those connected words into big ideas and run them through the SCAMPER checklist before you start sketching possible design executions.

Picture Association

This is another kind of mind mapping that relies on pictures as a source of raw material.

1. Print out photographs and illustrations that feel related to the project. This can include material from online image search engines, design inspiration resources and magazines, art books, stock web sites and image bookmarking web sites like FFFFOUND! (ffffound.com).

2. Arrange your images in groups or clusters that seem to speak to one another, then write words around the clusters that describe the essential messages they convey.

3. From these groups, distill your findings into possible directions or design sketches and run them through the SCAMPER checklist before sketching full execution ideas.

Brutethink

This brainstorming technique is included in the book *Thinkertoys* by Michael Michalko, and it's good to use at times when you're really stuck. Human beings have a tendency to find relationships between things whose meanings seem to be in direct conflict. The tension between those sparring words or images, and the ensuing friction in your mind, forms the sparks that can ignite more novel concepts.

1. Come up with a seed word related to the overall project (or an old one that you couldn't get to "activate").
2. Write down the first random thing that pops into your mind.
3. Hold both words in your mind, then find as many ways as possible to (intuitively) associate the idea and the random word. See what words, images and overarching concepts begin to emerge.

Idea Inversion

If you've been brainstorming and none of your ideas inspire you, try this method. Take a concept that's not quite working and envision its exact opposite in every way. Write out the opposing attributes, and draw that new idea. Compare the new idea to what you started with, then mix and match elements from both to inspire new possibilities.

Free-Form Sketching

Draw pictures, words and layout ideas in a free-form, associative way. Every five minutes, step back, assess and refocus on an element on the page that suggests further possibilities. This method often inspires new possibilities when you work with another designer and swap your notebooks mid-brainstorm.

Design Role Playing

In tandem with another designer, friend or relative, act out how your client's product or service could be used in the real world. Observe, react and question your behavior in order to glean insight from the experience and inspire possible design ideas. This method is very effective in helping people to envision design ideas for novel products or interactive experiences.

Yes, And...

Provide a group with a problem to solve. The first person who comes up with a possible solution shares it

One of my classes used Design Role Playing to help solve the Touch Screen of Deaf Rock challenge. See page 209.

with the group. Then, go around the room clockwise and continue to evolve that solution without judgment by saying, "Yes, and," then adding to it. Have one person record the solutions as the group morphs the original idea into something new. When the evolved idea returns to its original maker, consider ways to invert the idea and see what happens. I observed this method in a collaborative brainstorm led by Steve Portigal at a design conference.

Designer Mad Libs

You know that game Mad Libs, where you fill in the blanks with words? Create a simple Mad Lib for your project that describes your concept. Your Mad Lib could be phrased like this: My _____ is like _____ because _____. Try writing different words in the blanks and see what stories emerge. Or ask random people to fill in the blanks and work from their ideas.

Future Thinking

Stop brainstorming in the here and now and start exploring the future. If your project concepts were going to appear one year in the future, what would they look like? Removing the constraint of what's possible from a real-world standpoint can sometimes give you more space to roam in a design exploration.

Blank Bubbles

Sketch your target audience like they're in a cartoon, complete with empty speech balloons and potential activities that they might be taking part in. Add dialogue to the speech balloons, just like you're writing a comic book. What kind of story is this person telling you? This also works well if you put a picture of your intended audience in a photo frame on your desk, then place sticky notes around it with possible things they are saying to you. You can keep the photo for the life of the design project, changing the dialogue as the project evolves.

Don't Draw—Use Design Sketching

Design sketching isn't formal drawing or illustration. It's a way to rapidly record and explore visual ideas.

Many of us learned to draw things beautifully in a photorealistic way. This is often considered a cost of entry for being a designer. As each of us learned to draw, we evolved our own style and approach as to how we rendered elements in an illustration. These drawing habits can increase the expressiveness of what peers up at us from the page. But using our illustration skills for sketching designs can lead to overestimating the quality of the idea itself. The quality of your sketch should never hide a weak idea.

By using rough design sketching as you tackle the challenges in this book, you can quickly consider layout and grid use, select type styles and applications, determine the art direction of photography and illustration, and draft copy for your final execution, all before you even come near a computer. Even the most adept Adobe Photoshop artists and Illustrator whiz kids need to do some form of preplanning when under deadline. Most design ideas can be iterated more quickly on paper.

Being aware of the fidelity of your design sketching can have a big impact on the speed at which you can render ideas, as well as the number of ideas you can place on the page. If you take too much time polishing a single idea in a sketch, you may miss a better idea that decided not to wait around for you to finish.

Also, please visit CreativeWorkshopTheBook.com for more challenges, downloadable worksheets, and a free teacher's guide for classroom and corporate use.

SAY HELLO TO THE DESIGNRANDOMIZER™

If you want to make these challenges even harder, try using the DesignRandomizer. It's a feedback generator that will teach you how to handle arbitrary client changes in your design work.

Photocopy this page, then cut on the dotted lines and throw all the slips of paper into a hat. When you're half-way through executing one of your design challenges, draw a slip of paper from the hat and do what it says.

See if you can stay nimble in the face of shifting client needs and still yield a meaningful result in the finished design!

Make the logo bigger. Twice as big.	(Identify the main color used in your design.) We don't use that color.
Add two more columns to your page grid.	If it's photography, use illustration. (Or vice versa.)
You're just wrong. Start over with another concept from your brainstorm.	The CEO's wife would prefer a handwritten font.
Use purple as the anchor color in your design.	Cut the copy in half. Then cut it in half again.
You know what your design needs? Skydivers.	Over budget. Cut your color scheme to black and white.
Use circles in the background of your design.	Hard drive failed! Complete your design without a computer.
Add twenty years to your target audience.	Make things feel more "edgy."
Tone it down. Make the whole layout more conservative.	Can the photography or illustration you chose "pop" more?
I bet this would look great in 3-D. Give it more dimension.	Change the orientation of your design 90 degrees.
Spend only twenty minutes finishing this design.	This should really be a web site. (If it's already a web site, make it a poster.)

Introduction

FOUNDATION

Go back to basics. Brand yourself. Real-world typography. Delve into design history. When you are finished with the test, put down your pencil. Think in white space. Reading blue. Grids, grids, grids. Embrace your inner juvenile delinquent. Using five typefaces is just plain evil. Now destroy the font. Scientific branding. Hand-drawn, yet refined. Different angles on one photo. A hundred design ideas in just one hour.

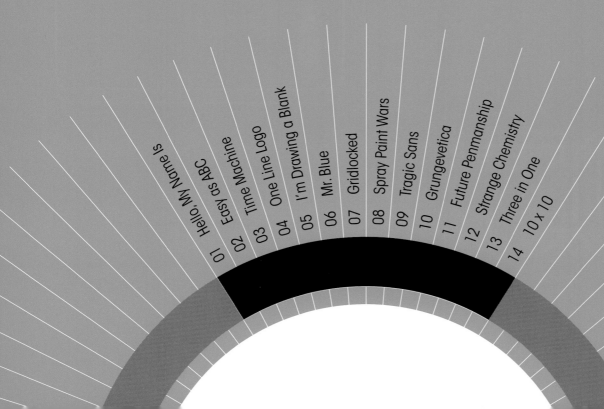

Hello, My Name Is

 30 minutes   Identity development, illustration

My trash can overflows with crumpled-up sketches. On my desktop is a folder jam-packed with Illustrator files of lovingly executed logos composed of delicate, hand-finessed Bézier curves. It's been almost three months, and no matter how many times I try to design for this client, I'm just not satisfied with the work.

This is a branding assignment for… well… me.

Identity development is the most poetic of the design disciplines, where all excess is pared away to reveal the pure essence of a client's brand. But when it comes to self-promotion, most designers can't easily gain the self-detachment necessary to summarize their own practice in an artful mark. (And without spending eons on the result.) That's what makes this first challenge a form of self-help.

> *"Designing for yourself is worse than representing a client; it can be like having an identity crisis."*
>
> —AIGA's *Graphic Design: A Career Guide and Education Directory*

CHALLENGE

Spend ten minutes answering the following questions: "What are my three strengths as a designer? My weaknesses? What's my favorite color? What designers do I love? What design work do I enjoy? What kind of work do I want to do in the future?" Then design a logo for yourself that is clearly informed by your off-the-cuff responses. Be sure to stick to the time limit provided—don't cheat!

TAKE IT FURTHER

In a second thirty-minute period, explore how you can apply your logo to a stationery system, a brochure and a personal web site.

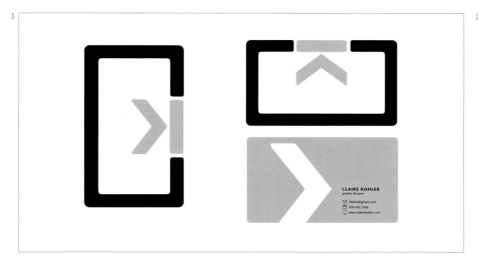

1 This identity concept for Claire Kohler, a designer based in Seattle, came out of a productive twenty-minute class brainstorm where she turned the initials of her name into a "fast-forward" icon that could be used on business cards, stationery and other elements of a self-promotional identity system.

2,3 In the same brainstorming period, Mark Notermann designed this simple mark for his design services. "I started by just making some diagonal lines. The inspiration was originally in the shape of a lightning bolt, which quickly became a factory icon. I liked the factory icon, and felt it represented industry and workmanship… I chose a 'safety yellow' to keep with the industrial theme but keep the palette light and lively. If I'm lucky, it says 'he likes to work hard but still has fun.'"

4 If this challenge freezes you in your tracks, try to design a logo for another designer. Jake Rae, a Seattle-area designer interested in specializing in brand and identity work, answered the questions associated with this challenge. Over twenty minutes, I brainstormed a number of possible logo solutions—this one being the most appropriate for his area of interest.

Easy as ABC

 120 minutes   Illustration, paper engineering, physical prototyping, photography, type design

When considering how we create typefaces, our methods of production have evolved considerably. From scratching symbols in the dirt to painting letterforms, we have developed increasingly sophisticated tools to communicate with written language.

But it wasn't until the invention of movable type that the discipline of typography truly began to coalesce. And yet, even with this vast array of tools at our disposal, from the pencil to the computer, unlimited typefaces still exist beyond the printed page—in the physical world.

CHALLENGE

Design a typeface that will be composed from elements in the world around you. Assemble your twenty-six-character alphabet using only found objects or environments. Letters may be documented through collage, photography, photocopying, digital illustration and other appropriate mediums. Avoid examples of computer typefaces out "in the wild," documenting elements of existing writing or signage, or pulling into your typeface anything that may be considered a traditional letterform.

"Letters are highly specialized images, and we have always read words as images. Words are perceived as silhouette image-shapes; the letters they are made from are actually little pictures, and writing is a highly evolved and specialized form of drawing."

—Timothy Donaldson, *Shapes for Sounds*

TAKE IT FURTHER

Add in numbers, symbols and supplementary punctuation as part of your real-world font. Or create a poster that shows your lettering in action.

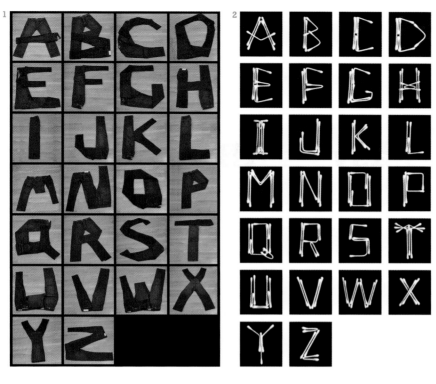

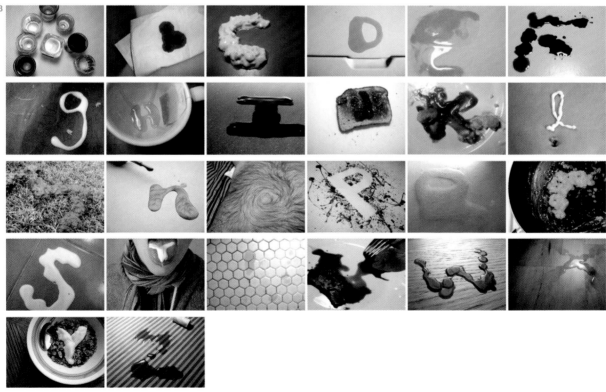

1 For this found alphabet, Donnie Dinch stood on a chair in his bedroom and arranged his jeans in concert with his girlfriend's jeans to create his own "Denim Alphabet."

2 Exploring the bathroom for type-design inspiration, Jessica Thrasher landed upon a box of Q-tips® as the ingredients for a very soft and absorbent "Q-tip Alphabet."

3 In Claire Kohler's "Liquid Alphabet," letterforms are constructed from various fluids. For example, the letter *H* is made from honey, while the *V* is implied by leftover balsamic vinegar from an eaten salad. See if you can determine which liquids were used for each letter.

Time Machine

 90 minutes Research, print advertising

We study art history more thoroughly than advertising history. The best art is crafted to withstand the ravages of decades, while the best advertising is designed to linger in your mind after you toss aside the most recent issue of your favorite magazine—and hopefully reach for your computer to pull up Amazon.com.

But there is much to be learned from studying advertisements from a previous decade. A single ad can be a treasure trove of information about how tastes, products and societal norms have changed over time, giving a designer a valuable window into the consumer mind. So hit the fast-forward button on an old ad and rocket it into the future!

CHALLENGE

Select a print ad from before 1980 that you admire, then redesign it in a contemporary style as a full-page color ad for one of the following magazines: *Wired; GQ; Better Homes and Gardens; O, The Oprah Magazine; Dwell; Vanity Fair; or US Weekly.* Feel free to reinterpret the photography, illustration, copy and typography as necessary to match today's design idiom. For further inspiration and samples to draw from, explore Taschen's *Golden Age of Advertising* series. There are also stock libraries that can serve as a research tool.

"When one looks back at ads they seem hopelessly dated and often ineffectual. Let's face it, advertising today is all about being current, or even ahead of the curve. So why look at what is behind the times? ... Believe it or not, great advertising is also an intellectual enterprise. Little is haphazard about it, though it often seems so casual, often whimsical, even anti-intellectual."

—James B. Twitchell, *Twenty Ads That Shook the World*

TAKE IT FURTHER

If you want to stretch your design and illustration skills, try the same assignment in reverse: Find a print ad that you admire in a contemporary magazine, then redesign it as if it were created before 1980.

Lemon.

The closest you'll get to a real lemon is the color.
VW inspectors run each car through a barrage of tests, and say 'no' to one out of fifty.

The world's slowest Macintosh.

Suddenly, everyone is talking about personal computers. Are you ready for one?

Macintosh

1 Care to redesign one of the industry-defining, classic Volkswagen ads from the 1950s? Montreal-based book designer Michel Vrana kept the spirit of the original "Lemon" ad by DDB, only needing to update the car and a little dollop of copy.

2 Donnie Dinch took a classic advertisement by Apple for the launch of the original Macintosh and brought it into the future—while cleverly forgetting to bring the computer along for the ride. Would you like to get your hands on the slowest Macintosh ever?

3 "I don't know about you, but I've been looking for one of those newfangled Model T automobiles…" Designer Jake Rae took a tongue-in-cheek approach to this challenge.

The New Ford Model T

Bringing style back into the way you drive

 **One Line Logo**

 30 minutes   Identity

An owl clinging to a tree branch. A woman's face, framed by a dove. The whimsical shape of a painter's loyal dachshund…

When leafing through the collected pencil sketches of Pablo Picasso, it's easy to be inspired by his fluid use of line. By reducing each visual idea to a single line recorded on a sheet of paper, he was able to explore a wealth of artistic possibilities.

With the following challenge, try to capture the same free-form illustrative gesture in your own design work.

"Art is the elimination of the unnecessary."
—Pablo Picasso

 CHALLENGE

You've been asked to submit an identity design for the 2012 Olympic Games in London. The initial sketch of your logo must be composed from a single, unbroken line. Once you've placed your pen or pencil down on the paper, you can't take it off the page until the logo is complete. Don't go back for corrections—embrace mistakes!

TAKE IT FURTHER

For a further challenge, try this exercise with two or more designers. Each person is allowed to make one line on the page, and then must pass the pencil to the next person to continue the thought. Use colored pencils to further enhance the process.

1,2,3 Meta Newhouse, principal of Newhouse Design and a graphic design professor at Montana State University, took on this challenge "because it was an odd way to go about designing a logo… I typically do some research—review visual imagery, competitive marks, learn everything I can about the client, etc.—then I sit down and do quite a bit of writing… But the rules were the rules, so I started drawing one-stroke doodles in my notebook. I did begin with the idea of a flame/torch, as that was the only thing I felt I could accomplish with one continuous line, and I felt the line had to represent *something* that communicated Olympics. This was a fairly foreign process for me, as I really don't think I draw all that well, but it was interesting to see that some of the drawings worked better than others, and why. For example, there is a drawing with subtle loops at the tips of the flames, which sort of look like sparks, or little flames shooting up from those tips. I thought that was a bit of serendipity. So, I kept going, drawing, drawing, drawing. I experimented with the flames shooting up in descending order, and… the image began to lean more and more to the right. A few started to look less like flames and more like some kind of dove/bird. And then my writing mind took over and started thinking about what the Olympics are all about. Sure, they are about athleticism, excellence and endurance, but since so many different countries participate, it is also about community—appreciating each other's differences but also our similarities. So the dove symbol really started to make sense to me. I would never have gotten to that if I had stuck with my old tried-and-true process."

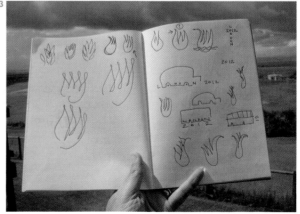

4

4 Jake Rae and Katharine Widdows took this challenge further, creating this logo together over the course of twenty minutes: the crown and the sweatband, happy together.

5 Erik Borreson's approach to this challenge was to have Big Ben, the Olympic torch and the word "London" as part of one single line.

5

I'm Drawing a Blank

 60 minutes   Collateral

White space… the final frontier.

These are the voyages of the graphic designer. Our mission: to bring balance and grace to an otherwise overloaded layout. To seek out opportunities to pare away excess and focus on what's necessary. To boldly convey the appropriate conceptual idea to our audience.

Our quest for bold use of white space is what makes the following challenge so difficult—and the results that come out of it so rewarding.

"The single most overlooked element in visual design is emptiness."

—Alexander W. White, *The Elements of Graphic Design: Space, Unity, Page Architecture, and Type*

CHALLENGE

You were recently hired by a paint company to help them with a rebranding effort. For your first project, they would like you to design a 9" x 12" (23cm x 30cm) folder that will hold a revamped press kit and other supplementary collateral. Your client has given only one mandatory direction: The folder must have at least 90 percent white showing in the overall design.

TAKE IT FURTHER

Once you've completed the folder, determine how you can design a set of sales sheets that describe the characteristics of various lines of paint. Your sell sheets should clearly associate with the cover and feel integrated with your proposed brand aesthetic.

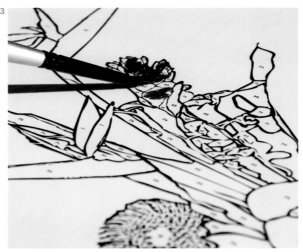

1

2

1   MUSTARD YELLOW
2   FIELD GREEN
3   GRASSY GREEN
4   SWEET ORANGE
5   LIPSTICK RED
6   LIGHT LAVENDER
7   DEEP PURPLE
8   SLATE BLUE

3

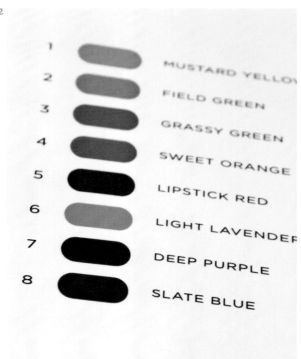

1,2,3 In a twenty-minute brainstorm session for this challenge, I sketched out an idea for a paint-by-numbers cover for the fictional Kingston Artist's Supply catalog. The reader can flatten out the folder, purchase the paint colors noted in the legend on the back cover and start on their first masterwork.

4,5,6 A quick design sketch can express a visual idea just as thoroughly as a final, polished drawing. While brainstorming solutions to this challenge within a twenty-minute time limit, Jake Rae (4), Michelle Cormack (5) and Katharine Widdows (6) and all came up with simple, viable ideas that imply a range of possible design executions.

Mr. Blue

⏱ 60 minutes   ✳ Magazine design

Blue is America's most popular color. There are so many variations on this hue—from the sparkle of a sapphire to the clear blue sky, the deep cerulean ocean to the stunning iris at the tip of a peacock feather.

This challenge is about how many different ways you can interpret the color blue.

CHALLENGE

Design the masthead and the cover of a new magazine devoted solely to things that are associated with the *idea* of blue. Consider the magazine name, suggestions for art direction and what kinds of articles you think the editor should include.

Don't restrict yourself to literal interpretation— feel free to branch your design ideas out into what kinds of people, places, feelings, artworks or emotions may be conceptually related to the color.

> *"Artists can color the sky red because they know it's blue. Those of us who aren't artists must color things the way they really are or people might think we're stupid."*
>
> —Jules Feiffer

TAKE IT FURTHER

Move beyond the masthead and cover of your first issue. Design the magazine's grid and put together two sample spreads, including the table of contents and the first spread of your favorite article concept.

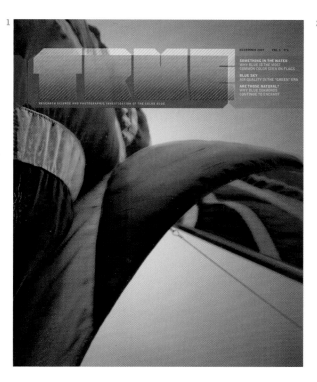

1 Mark Notermann's magazine concept is *True*: a scientific and photographic exploration of the color blue. Inside its pages, you'll find articles about how the color blue is the most frequently used color on flags, explorations into air quality and why blue diamonds continue to enchant us.

2 Jake Rae designed *Carver,* a magazine devoted to the surfing life. Get stoked about surfing the Gulf Coast or head out to Hawaii to check out the Banzai Pipeline.

3 Michelle Cormack used a literary slant on the idea of blue with the invention of *Blu,* Canada's literary review magazine dedicated to symptoms of loneliness and heartache. With this issue, read up on Canada's country music scene, enjoy the short fiction of Bob Thompson and take up a search for the real Richard Wilbur.

3

blu

canada's literary review magazine dedicated to symptoms of loneliness and heartache

volume 6 :: issue 5 :: july 2009 :: i'll take the holy vow of being worthless

14 gloom, despair and agony on me: canada's country music

23 i don't need compassion: short fiction from bob thompson

36 a finished man: searching for the real richard wilbur

hairline fracture amy clampitt

it was as though we watched the hairline fracture
of the quotidian widen to a geomorphic fissure,
its canyon edge bridged by the rainbows of a terror
that nothing would ever again be right
between us, that wherever we went, nowhere
in the universe would the bone again be knit
or the rift be closed.

4 My obsession with digital collage artwork and birds led to the invention of the art magazine *Blubird*.

5 Jessica Thrasher's contribution was *Bleu*, a magazine where you can explore "sea life under a scope." Take a dive into issue #24 and learn all about jellyfish, including their current overabundance in today's waters and Japan's latest craze: jellyfish ice cream.

6 Designer Subarna Ghoshal used a photograph of a blue vase in her house as a foundation for a wide-ranging exploration of color, emotion and impression.

Gridlocked

 60 minutes Layout

"All design work involves problem solving on both visual and organizational levels," says designer and educator Timothy Samara. Without understanding how to use a grid as the basis of your page layout decisions, you aren't likely to master the skill of artful organization.

Use the following challenge as a way to safely explore the possibilities for page layout that exist when using a grid system.

> *"As the use of grids has changed from self-conscious gesture to that of second-nature reflex, so, too, has the viewing public become more accustomed to information presented to them in greater quantities, simultaneously, in greater complexity, and in more languages. And they're not simply accustomed to it: They want it that way."*
>
> —Timothy Samara, *Making and Breaking the Grid*

TAKE IT FURTHER

Repeat this same exercise. Each time you try it, there will be new layout problems to conquer.

CHALLENGE

You've been tasked with designing the interior spread of an 11" x 17" (28 cm x 43 cm) brochure, 8½" x 11" (22 cm x 28 cm) folded, for a juvenile diabetes treatment plan. After you've determined the name of the treatment plan and a logo for it, design the brochure spread as follows:

1. Roll a die to determine the number of columns in your grid on the left and right pages of your spread.

2. Based on that grid, design your spread with the following six required elements: 1 picture (3" x 4" [8 cm x 10 cm]), 4–6 paragraphs of copy (500 words), 1 paragraph legal (100 words in tiny type), 1 inset/pull quote (20 words), 1 headline (8 words), and your logo (shown at least 1.25" [3 cm] wide).

3. Create a new version of the same spread where the logo is at least 2" (5 cm) larger in width. How does that change your layout?

4. Roll your die again and add that number of columns to your page grid. Then reorganize the page content to fit that new grid. What in your design needs to change to fit the new arrangement, while also accommodating your oversized logo?

1

1,2,3,4 After creating his logo, designer Jake Rae rolled a two on his die and created a first layout for his brochure with a simple two-column grid. He then increased his logo size, which forced him to rethink the placement of nearly every page element in his first layout. When he rolled the die again, he came up with a three, which forced him to redesign the layout again with an awkward number of columns for the type of content on the page—plus a gigantic logo.

2

Diabetes develops due to a diminished production of insulin (in type 1) or resistance to its effects (in type 2 and gestational). Both lead to hyperglycemia, which largely causes the acute signs of diabetes: excessive urine production, resulting compensatory thirst and increased fluid intake, blurred vision, unexplained weight loss, lethargy, and changes in energy metabolism.

All forms of diabetes have been treatable since insulin became medically available in 1921, but there is no cure. The injections by a syringe, insulin pump, or insulin pen deliver insulin, which is a basic treatment of type 1 diabetes. Type 2 is managed with a combination of dietary treatment, exercise, medications and insulin supplementation.

Diabetes and its treatments can cause many complications. Acute complications including hypoglycemia, ketoacidosis, or nonketotic hyperosmolar coma may occur if the disease is not adequately controlled. Serious long-term complications include cardiovascular disease, chronic renal failure, retinal damage, which can lead to blindness, several types of

Opening doors
for the lives of our future

All forms of diabetes have been treatable since insulin became medically available in 1921, but there is no cure.

Diabetes mellitus, often referred to simply as diabetes , is a syndrome of disordered metabolism, usually due to a combination of hereditary and environmental causes, resulting in abnormally high blood sugar levels (hyperglycemia). Blood glucose levels are controlled by a complex interaction of multiple chemicals and hormones in the body, including the hormone insulin made in the beta cells of the pancreas. Diabetes mellitus refers to the group of diseases that lead to high blood glucose levels due to defects in either insulin secretion or insulin action in the body.

nerve damage, and microvascular damage, which may cause erectile dysfunction and poor wound healing. Poor healing of wounds, particularly of the feet, can lead to gangrene, and possibly to amputation. Adequate treatment of diabetes, as well as increased emphasis on blood pressure control and lifestyle factors such as not smoking and maintaining a healthy body weight, may improve the risk profile of most of the chronic complications. In the developed world, diabetes is the most significant cause of adult blindness in the non-elderly and the leading cause of non-traumatic amputation in adults, and diabetic nephropathy is the main illness requiring renal dialysis in the United States.

3

Opening doors
for the lives of our future

All forms of diabetes have been treatable since insulin became medically available in 1921, but there is no cure.

4

Opening doors
for the lives of our future

All forms of diabetes have been treatable since insulin became medically available in 1921, but there is no cure.

Spray Paint Wars

 120 minutes   Hand animation,
identity development, typography

Remember the airbrush?

Until the advent of computer art, many commercial artists used this method of spray painting to create everything from food advertisements to retro pin-up girls to science-fiction book covers.

Fast-forward to today, and the vernacular has been limited to graffiti—or to the virtual airbrush in Photoshop. It's rare that you'll see a designer on the street, practicing his trade with a can in hand.

With this in mind, stretch your hand-typography skills by taking on the following challenge.

> *"People say graffiti is ugly, irresponsible and childish. But that's only if it's done properly."*
> —Banksy

CHALLENGE

Come up with a name for a new clothing company whose work is inspired by street art, then design a logo for your company in a graffiti style. Once the logo is complete, create a motion graphics storyboard where your logo will be painted into place on a television within the store.

TAKE IT FURTHER

Put together a storyboard showing a "graffiti battle ad" between your company and a competing street wear company as part of an event going on next month at a rap battle. The highlight of the event is two different graffiti artists fighting for supremacy and layering upon each other's work.

1,2 Brandon Dawley took a different tack, working his hand lettering into a full graffiti tag that would look quite comfortable on a clothing store sign.

3,4,5 Richard Wallace started with a word list of what a shopper might find at his store—shoes, clothes, high tops, hoodies and so on—which led to the name Manrs. He then conducted a range of type explorations in his sketchbook (3): "In drawing the logo I realized that it could be built from a series of repeated lines (4), and went into the storyboards with that in mind." His final storyboard (5) feels fashionable, with the raking repeated lines providing great contrast with the splashy spray-painted backdrop.

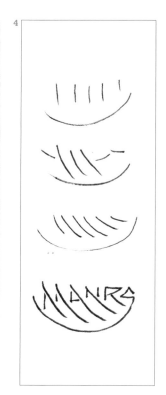

Exercise 08

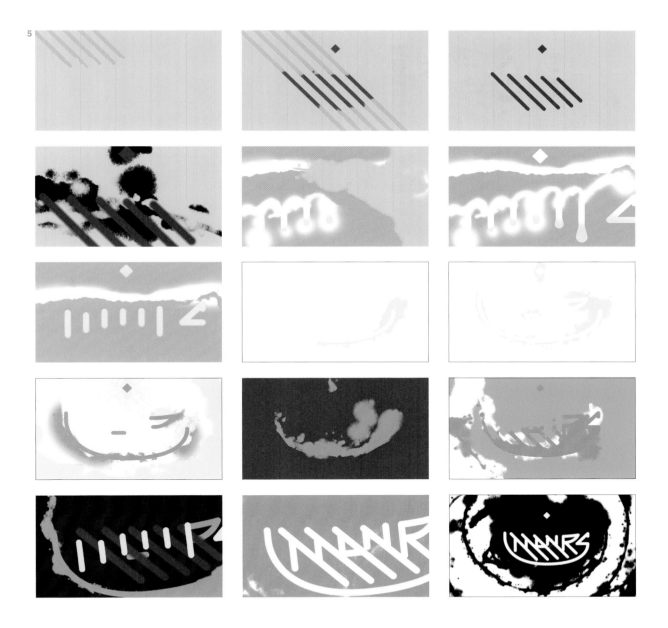

Tragic Sans

 30 minutes   Collateral, research, typography

If you are a student of typography, you know the more important rules of thumb for good typesetting.

Be sure to kern your headlines. In most cases, keep your paragraphs in a rag right alignment. Limit the number of fonts on a page so your layout doesn't turn into a total circus.

With this challenge, you're going to break that last rule. Who doesn't like a circus?

CHALLENGE

Create a brochure cover promoting the Slow Food movement. As part of your design, you must use five or more unique fonts. Can you make a coherent brochure cover under these constraints?

"If one more wannabe David Carson shows me one more unreadable headline with five different fonts in it without there being any reason for the five fonts or the lack of readability, I fear I may spit up."

—Mark Fenske

TAKE IT FURTHER

Design a brochure holder that can display your collateral piece in a grocery store. In your work, be sure to incorporate two more fonts that weren't part of the original brochure.

CHEW ON THIS:
☞ IT'S THE SLOW FOOD MANIFESTO

OUR CENTURY, WHICH BEGAN AND HAS DEVELOPED UNDER THE INSIGNIA OF INDUSTRIAL CIVILIZATION, FIRST INVENTED THE MACHINE AND THEN TOOK IT AS ITS LIFE MODEL. WE ARE ENSLAVED BY SPEED AND HAVE ALL SUCCUMBED TO THE SAME INSIDIOUS VIRUS: FAST LIFE, WHICH DISRUPTS OUR HABITS, PERVADES THE PRIVACY OF OUR HOMES AND FORCES US TO EAT FAST FOODS. TO BE WORTHY OF THE NAME, HOMO SAPIENS SHOULD RID HIMSELF OF SPEED BEFORE IT REDUCES HIM TO A SPECIES IN DANGER OF EXTINCTION. A FIRM DEFENSE OF QUIET MATERIAL PLEASURE IS THE ONLY WAY TO OPPOSE THE UNIVERSAL FOLLY OF FAST LIFE. MAY SUITABLE DOSES OF GUARANTEED SENSUAL PLEASURE AND SLOW, LONG-LASTING ENJOYMENT PRESERVE US FROM THE CONTAGION OF THE MULTITUDE WHO MISTAKE FRENZY FOR EFFICIENCY.

Don't worry. We have a plan!

Our first defense should begin at the table with Slow Food. Let us rediscover the flavors and savors of regional cooking and banish the degrading effects of Fast Food. In the name of Productivity, Fast Life has changed our way of being and threatens our environments and our landscapes.

SO SLOW FOOD IS NOW THE ONLY TRULY PROGRESSIVE ANSWER.

That is what real culture is all about: developing taste rather than demeaning it. And what better way to set about this than an international exchange of experiences, knowledge, projects?

WANT TO LEARN MORE? WELL THEN, JUST TURN THE PAGE.

☞ SLOW FOOD GUARANTEES A BETTER FUTURE.

1 For this challenge, Michelle Cormack decided to use the entire Slow Food Manifesto as her brochure cover. By chunking the text into multiple type sizes and fonts, the reader's eye must slow down and take it all in. The use of earthy green and brown-red hues, used in association with sky blue, seems reminiscent of old-fashioned theater and vaudeville posters.

2 Katharine Widdows took the negativity inherent in the use of multiple fonts and turned it to her advantage—conveying what we may sacrifice daily in the name of convenience.

3 Drawing from the rustic Italian origins of the Slow Food movement, Mark Notermann's design weaves five fonts together in a manner that has a slow pace, an elegant feel and a handcrafted polish that feels intentional, not haphazard.

Grungevetica

 120 minutes ✳ Type design

"Watching me work is like watching a refrigerator make ice," said Matthew Carter, creator of classic type-faces such as the omnipresent Verdana. Such is the price of perfection: your body hunched over a draft-ing table with pencil, paper and protractor, belabor-ing the counter shape in the letter *q* for days on end…

Designing a legible typeface is a painstaking process yielding a product that, if properly executed, is entirely transparent to readers. In this regard, Helvetica is the undisputed king of the type world—entirely neutral to the eye. No one seems to have been able to beat Helvetica for sheer ubiquity.

So, for this challenge, let's distress this notion of typog-raphy as a perfectionist pursuit. Let's burn Helvetica to the ground and watch the phoenix that rises from its ashes.

> *"Any good typeface can be completely destroyed when misused or exten-sively overused. Helvetica seemed to sustain a beat-ing like no other."*
> —Alexander Gelman

CHALLENGE

Project yourself far into the future. Linotype GmbH has chosen you to create a seventieth anni-versary edition of Helvetica—a modern update of the font composed of destroyed letterforms. What would the twenty-six characters of this new font look like? How would you associate your work to the legacy of the original face?

TAKE IT FURTHER

Design a poster for your new typeface release, writing eye-catching copy to convey the ideas underlying your solution.

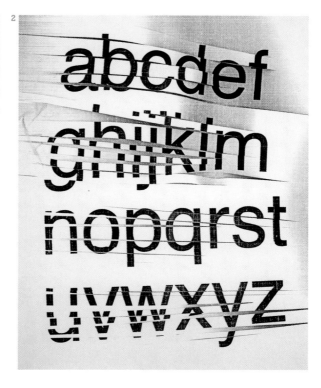

1 Book designer Michel Vrana says of his font Feedback: "This is my grunge 'cover' of Helvetica... I gravitated toward photocopy manipulation as a basis for my exploration, as a visual nod to the photocopied band posters that would have been used during the '90s... In layering the three different manipulations with transparent cyan, magenta and yellow, the resulting [letterforms] brought out the Helvetica-ness of each version, with some fun outer-edge 'feedback' still apparent."

2 How much can you cut up a typeface and still have it be legible? This page is from a series of experiments by Katharine Widdows and Jessica Thrasher where they explored methods of font surgery.

3 Michelle Cormack and Shimon Alkon made Helvetica grungy through deconstruction, giving each letter of the alphabet a completely different hand-wrought visual treatment.

4,5,6 Jake Rae and I created Nope, a variant of Helvetica that is a scribbled version of the original face. In the process of creating Nope we discovered that the indentations left by our heavy scribbles, as well as the interactions between our tracing paper and the printed font, would make lovely motifs for further exploration.

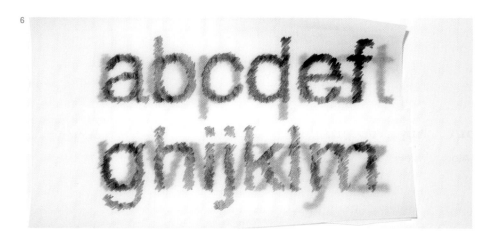

Exercise 10

Future Penmanship

⏱ 90 minutes   ✳ Illustration, identity development, research

A physics graduate student once told me that the universe is expanding at an impossibly fast rate—and at some later date, it may collapse back in on itself, recreating the Big Bang.

"What are the odds that such a thing could happen?" I said.

"Well, that depends on what scientific point of view you choose," he said. Then he began to outline a series of fascinating theories that, to this very day, I still can't remember.

Does this mean he was a bad communicator? Or that I just didn't grasp the concepts he had brought to bear on our conversation? In the world of design, if we don't clarify and communicate complex ideas in the simplest ways possible, our efforts are considered failures.

So, what do we do when tasked to communicate an idea that's impossibly complex? And in a manner that's artistically counterintuitive? With this challenge, you'll stretch the boundaries of both your mind and your making skills.

> ### *"A perfection of means, and confusion of aims, seems to be our main problem."*
>
> —Albert Einstein

CHALLENGE

A technology startup focused on the area of quantum computing wants you to help craft their new brand system. They're too busy chasing venture capital to explain to you what quantum computing actually is, so you'll need to do a bit of research to understand what they're technically pursuing. And, while they don't care what name you come up with, they did have some mandatory input regarding the way in which you render their logo: They want all elements of the system to be rendered in a hand-wrought calligraphic style. Can you design a logo in this fashion—saying bleeding-edge technology with a nibbed fountain pen and ink?

TAKE IT FURTHER

How would your design explorations manifest themselves through a Flash advertisement? On your client's web site? In a complete stationery system?

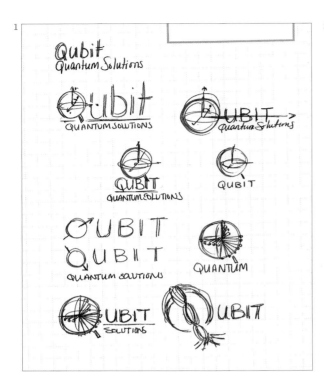

1,2,3 Manda Szewczyk settled on the name Qubit for her identity—which is short for "quantum bit," a unit of quantum information. In receiving her sketches of potential mark ideas and her final logo (which was accompanied by thorough color studies), I couldn't help but think that an intriguing way to execute on her logo as a complete brand system would be for the colors to vary depending on placement and use. So, on a web page, for example, the color of the logo could vary depending on any number of factors, such as time, date, weather, what buttons you're planning to click and so forth.

4 Designer and illustrator Lisa Stewart created this mark with the following rationale as its basis. "While quantum computing is still young, three fundamental properties are [its] basis—most of which are based on quantum mechanics. The physical representations extracted for the purpose of identity building were adopted from research and are defined [here]. The Optical Lattice & Bloch Sphere: The well of the optical lattice is represented by the calligraphic *U* and the corresponding atom is the sphere that hovers above. The sphere also represents the Bloch Sphere, the pure state space. Light and Sound: The three knots undulating horizontally represent light and sound waves. Once these elements were assigned, the arrangement humanizes the identity, promoting an entanglement of both quantum computing and data collection." I'm not sure I understand exactly what Lisa's talking about, but I think the client would be happy with the final design.

5 Erik Borreson took a type-only approach. "It is a hybrid of uncial and gothic calligraphy—based on my initial 'swoosh' form in the letter *I*."

12 Strange Chemistry

 90 minutes    Annual reports

I'm in awe of the mixologist at my favorite bar. She's always throwing wildly contrasting ingredients into her cocktails. Last night, I tried a Thai chile-infused vodka with muddled cucumber and passion fruit purée. Each visit yields something creative and new to my palate, and I'm always asking her to surprise me with bold new concoctions.

Hmm… I think I just described the designer-client relationship. When bringing a design concept to life, you want to foster the delicious friction that happens between opposing forces. Just like peanut butter and boysenberry jam on thick whole wheat bread, varying flavors and textures achieve greater substance when mashed together.

With the following challenge, you'll need to exploit incongruity to achieve an artistic effect—on multiple levels.

> *"You can take two substances, put them together, and produce something powerfully different (table salt), sometimes even explosive (nitroglycerine)."*
>
> —Diane Ackerman, *A Natural History of the Senses*

CHALLENGE

There's a new breed of chemical company out there in the wild that's seeking an ethical, "green" stance toward their efforts to produce critical substances that help today's industries function. You've been asked to create the annual report for one such company. The overall theme for this year is "Better Living Through Chemistry."

In order to complete this challenge, you need to first determine the name and brand position of this company—counter to all of their competitors in the market. Then, based on your proposed brand position, provide the client with a cover design and first spread that conveys their desired theme in a powerful manner. And as a requirement for your art direction, you must mix scruffy hand-drawn type with ultra-refined photography.

TAKE IT FURTHER

Consider how you could expand your print design into an online experience that would animate the visual and written themes in your report.

1 Regarding this design, Katharine Widdows said: "I formed the name of the company Organichem by fusing the words 'organic' and 'chemical,' which could be thought of as a paradox, or as a strategy for utilizing the best of both worlds. (I did find later that there does exist a chemical company with this name.) I wanted to balance images of natural, green growth with images of chemistry and lab work, and stress the idea of natural order and the order of thought and equations co-existing beautifully. In hindsight, it does seem important that the more 'natural' term forms the beginning of the name, as it is the precedent and basis for man-made chemicals."

2 In Michelle Cormack's annual report design for the fictional company NaturalElements, she notes that water is the most abundant chemical on Earth. As readers progress through the annual report, they would see each spread focus on another common chemical that forms a part of our everyday lives.

3 Designer Jake Rae's annual report cover for the fictional PrismaLab fuses photography and typography into one—and opens the door for mixing whiteboard marker sketch with photography through future spreads.

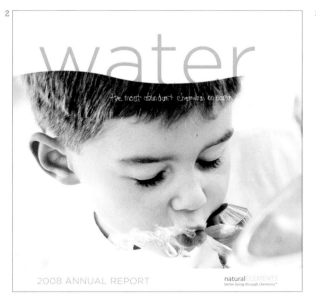

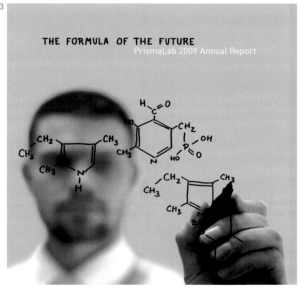

Three in One

 90 minutes   Photography, print advertising

While perusing a women's magazine, a print ad catches your eye. There's a happy woman picking dandelions with her young daughter, while the caption reads: "Because of cancer, Juliette's mother only has two months left to live."

A picture may be worth a thousand words, but sometimes it only takes a few words carefully selected by a designer to completely recast that picture's story. Coming up with compelling advertising concepts requires this kind of artful spin through the intelligent marriage of word and image. If executed properly, these ads hit you square in the gut.

Want some practice with this style of advertising? Take on the following challenge.

> ## "The secret of all effective advertising is not the creation of new and tricky words and pictures, but one of putting familiar words and pictures into new relationships."
> —Leo Burnett

CHALLENGE

Shoot a photograph of an item that you carry with you throughout the day. Then design three print ads showing that product in three different ways: positive, negative and metaphorical. As an example, if you took a photo of your eyeglasses, you could have a glowingly positive ad for the pair that you wear, an ad for a competing product that uses your glasses as an example of what not to buy, and a third ad that uses the glasses as an example of the focus you need when selecting a mutual fund. Be sure to preplan your ads in sketch form before moving into execution.

TAKE IT FURTHER

Make a storyboard for a TV ad adapted from your favorite ad from the sequence.

Memories. To go!

Stroller USB sticks are a great way to bring your memories everywhere
you go. Don't leave home without one. www.strollersticks.com

▦ stroller

Why take the risk?

Chances are you have a lot of important stuff on your computer. Financial
records. Email. Digital photos. Music... and more. If your backup system is
a memory stick, you're putting your data at risk. Musey is a simple and safe
way to back up all your important stuff. Your data is stored in a secure,
remote location, giving you peace of mind in the event of theft or disaster.
From $4.95 per month. Learn more at musey.com.

musey

If only it were
this easy to
cure memory loss.

It's easy to forget the little things.
But if memory loss is disrupting
your daily life, speak with your
doctor. It could be an early warning
sign of a more significant problem.

www.memoryloss.com

1,2,3 Designer Michelle Cormack
chose a USB memory stick as the
foundation of her three advertisements. For her positive ad, she
created a company called Stroller
whose USB sticks help you bring
your memories everywhere. In
her ad that focused on a negative attribute of the product, she
conceived of a cloud-based file
sharing service that could back up
all of your digital files—and then
arranged a photo shoot in her home
that showed the risks of leaving
copies of your data at large. And for
the ad that was meant to show the
product in a metaphorical context,
she used the USB stick as a literal
replacement for a woman's memory
in a public service announcement.

10 x 10

 90 minutes Packaging design

Ninety-eight… ninety-nine… one hundred sit-ups!

We force our bodies through all sorts of challenging workouts, but when it comes to exercising the mind, sustained ideation can leave a designer feeling completely spent. Plus, when I'm tasked with creating packaging concepts, I often feel like I'm running out of ideas after only a page or two of concentrated sketching.

As a general rule, I've found that this empty feeling is sheer illusion. The best way to dispel it is by forcing constant iteration and repetition in my sketchbook—especially when I don't think too hard about what my pencil is doing on the page. My best work often happens in this magical space.

Want to give it a try? In taking on this challenge, discover how to silence your inner critic by generating an astounding number of design ideas.

> **"Nothing is more dangerous than an idea when it's the only one you have."**
>
> —Émile Chartier, French philosopher

CHALLENGE

You've been hired by a soda company to create the packaging for an affordable organic energy drink. Your audience is well-off twenty-year-olds. Brainstorm a name and description of the drink, then spend sixty minutes on a hundred sketches of the possible energy drink design, including form factor and typography. Spend the last thirty minutes refining the hundred sketches down to three final design sketches that incorporate all of your best thinking.

TAKE IT FURTHER

Use the same process to create one hundred sketches outlining a web site design for your energy drink.

1,2 I spent ninety minutes on this challenge with an idea for an energy drink called tTree made with rooibos tea and enhanced with vitamins and minerals. As I reached sketch sixty, I began to realize that the name wasn't playing very well in my form factor ideas, so I began iterating the name with various design ideas, landing on Tsquared (or T² for short). By the time I had finished the initial sketching period, I had earmarked a few winners from the hundred thumbnail sketches that seemed worth pursing further, including a "message in a bottle" design that incorporated fruit leather or some other consumable object within the bottle that could be drawn out by the purchaser. Another idea that seemed interesting to pursue was a drink that, when the person opened the cap, released special flavorings into the tea that gave it an extra kick. And an idea that would probably get shot down by the FDA: an energy drink whose design mimicked prescription drug bottles.

2

3

4

5

3,4,5,6 Photocopy and cut out your favorite sketches, arranging and clustering them into bigger ideas. This is often the fastest way to get to the best result from the wide range of explorations that come from this challenge.

6

Exercise 14

EXECUTION

Get it done! One minute advertisement. Animate type meaningfully. Annual reports meet theater sports. Google your next project. Greatest hits illustration. Stories are kids' play. DIY philosophy. Beautify ugliness. "Unisex" shaving cream? Invent your own cereal. Your imagination, on DVD. Love monster movies. "Blink and you miss it" cinema. Three types of chocolate = endless possibilities. This ad dries clothes. Urban Gardening Web 2.0. Vacation in Saskatoon? Celebrate the idea of getting some sheep—I mean sleep.

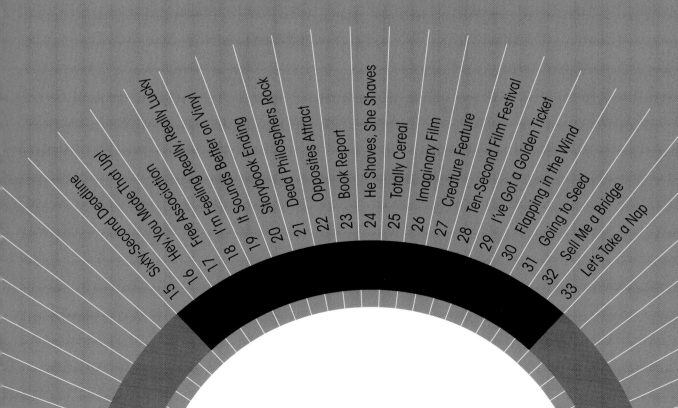

 **Sixty-Second Deadline**

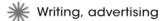

🕐 60 minutes 　 ✳ Writing, advertising

How long does it take to come up with a good idea? Answer: The time it takes you to reach your deadline.

No matter whether you have hours or minutes, a solid deadline will force you to cough up a great ad idea fast—and probably quicker than any other brainstorming method. In these kinds of hair-trigger creative situations, you learn to trust intuition and go with what feels right on the page.

Designers don't want to hear this, however. Don't great ideas materialize after you've agonized over the ninety-seventh iteration of your layout? Nope. In as little as one minute, creative lightning can strike. And in the process, that blank page before you can reveal a jewel of an idea.

In the following challenge, prepare yourself for the briefest of deadlines. You might be surprised at the results.

> *"Good work habits lead us to address specific problems systematically. Sometimes we even stumble upon a great idea along the way."*
>
> —Eric Karjaluoto

 CHALLENGE

Ask a friend or family member to fill a box with seven items from around his house. With a stopwatch at your side, randomly pick one item out of the box and take exactly sixty seconds to write a slogan that could be associated with the item. Do that for each item, sixty seconds each time. Then choose the most exceptional slogan from your rapid brainstorming and design a billboard for that product. Be sure to render your headline prominently in it.

TAKE IT FURTHER

See if you can repeat the same exercise to come up with a series of new headlines associated with the one in your billboard—which can then be used in print ads, posters and online advertising.

1

2

3

4

5

1,2,3,4 In true Burma-Shave style, designer Jessica Thrasher conceived of the slogans for this multi-part billboard series (in sixty seconds) that pays off the value of owning a multi-bit screwdriver. If the client was willing to pay a little extra in production, the screws could protrude from the billboard—providing extra dimension to the viewer on the road.

5 Jake Rae was provided with this stuffed dog toy and came up with the following slogan, which he then incorporated into a billboard ad for PrizeWinner Toys, a fictional company responsible for these obedient animals.

16

Hey, You Made That Up!

 60 minutes Motion graphics storyboarding, identity development

There are some things in life that can't be faked. Sugar in your morning coffee. Fresh-cut flowers in a crystal vase. Hair that hasn't been dyed, streaked or chemically treated within an inch of its life.

There are things in life that often seem faked, such as brand names for new products. We're surrounded by thousands of brands whose names are just empty containers. The ones that catch our attention often communicate their meaning through motion.

In the following challenge, put on your animator's hat and bring out the meaning in what could otherwise be meaningless.

> *"Brand is the F word of marketing. Everybody swears by it, few people are that good at it and everyone would like you to believe they do it more often than they do."*
>
> —Mark Di Soma

CHALLENGE

Write down three three-syllable adjectives. Create a new made-up word by mashing together the first syllable from the first adjective, the second syllable from the second, and the third from the third adjective. This is your client's new brand name. Apparently, they spent a billion dollars coming up with this name—the market research supports the choice—and as their designer, you're responsible for creating a six-panel storyboard for a motion graphics piece that will be shown at the shareholders' meeting.

The video should convey through typography, color and movement exactly what their company does in the market. Is this name describing a new product or service in the marketplace? A nonprofit initiative? Be as inventive as possible.

TAKE IT FURTHER

Write a voiceover script and select music to support your storyboard. Read the words out loud and time it to match up with your storyboard, noting what details you may not have considered as part of your motion graphics treatment.

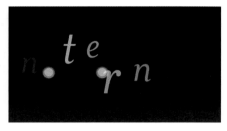

noteron
long life LED lights

1 In six frames, there isn't much time to tell a complex story. When I came up with Noteron, creator of energy-efficient LED lights for cars, this solution seemed to be the simplest way to express the benefit of their product. The lights had almost outlasted the car they were installed inside.

2 Mark Notermann chose the words "synchronized," "effortless" and "fantastic." That led to this simple storyboard for the Syncortic Pen, which can write on any surface.

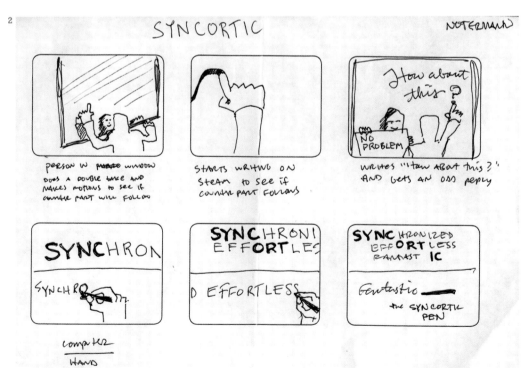

SYNCORTIC   NOTERMANN

PERSON W WINDOW DOES A DOUBLE TAKE AND MAKES MOTIONS TO SEE IF COUNTER PART WILL FOLLOW

STARTS WRITING ON STEAM TO SEE IF COUNTER PART FOLLOWS

WRITES "HOW ABOUT THIS?" AND GETS AN ODD REPLY

SYNCHRON

SYNCHRO

computer
HAND

SYNCHRONI
EFFORTLES

D EFFORTLESS

SYNC HRONIZED
EFFORTLESS
FANTAST IC

Fantastic
the SYNCORTIC PEN

Free Association

 60 minutes   ✳ Annual reports

Yes, I'd love to sit down and read your Form 10-K—as long as you include some beautiful charts, graphs and smiling children frolicking in a dandelion-laden meadow. And be sure to print the report on 100% recycled, post-consumer waste paper with soy inks on a printing press powered by wind.

Well, designing an annual report isn't *that* easy. Any designer who has lived through an annual report project knows the struggle of digesting a few dozen interviews with clients and customers and seeking that magical thread of story that will weave a full year of business and community activities into a cogent narrative. If you fail in making the story tangible in your overall copy and design, this long-form document becomes a jumble of disparate elements that lack a cohesive vision. Plus, as times grow tough for businesses and nonprofits, production values on the annual report receive the axe—further handcuffing your creative vision.

Never had a chance to design an annual report? Take this challenge and discover what it's like to summon a grand business narrative from seemingly random elements.

> *"Clients have no trouble paying $5,800 for an hour in a Gulfstream corporate jet or $425 for a month of parking. But God forbid they spend $3 per on a glossy annual report."*
>
> —Bill Cahan

CHALLENGE

Write down the name of an animal, a physical location somewhere in the world, and the name of a nonprofit you admire. Using this information, create the cover design of this year's annual report for said nonprofit, including some form of textual or visual reference to the animal and location. If you have time left, design the layout for the first and second spreads of the report, including considerations of the grid, while deftly weaving in the details you've improvised.

TAKE IT FURTHER

Take your annual report theme to the web. How would you extend the overall story of your project into an interactive experience that breaks free of the printed page?

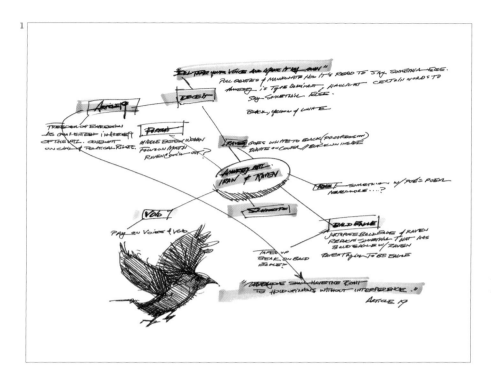

1,2 Designers Sean Baker from Pictoric and Lenny Vella from 'peeps creative tag-teamed this challenge. The client: Amnesty International. The target: Human rights and freedoms. The animal: Raven. Location: Iran. Using this seed material, the two designers used mind mapping to quickly generate ideas for their final execution.

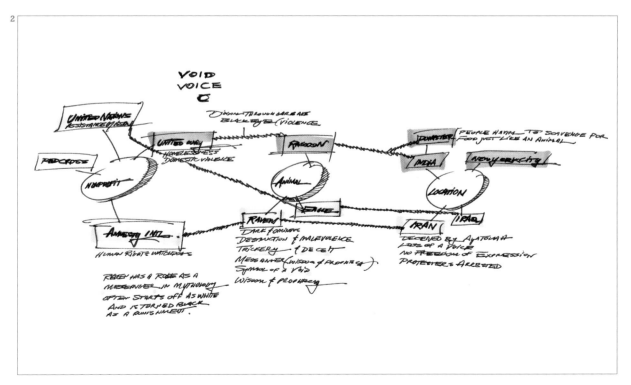

3,4 For the cover and spread of their annual report, Sean Baker and Lenny Vella utilized a type-only approach that highlights a portion of a speech by Mehdi Karroubi and Zahra Rahnavard to create a new message that speaks to Amnesty International's fight to protect the human rights of those who dissent with their governments.

I'm Feeling Really, Really Lucky

 90 minutes    User interface design

Mystery meat navigation. Flashing text. Jumbled page layouts. Frames. Awful photography. Amateur illustration. Overwritten copy—or the complete lack of words on the page. The list could go on and on.

The world is full of web sites that desperately need the loving attention of a visual designer. But our services are often engaged to create a site, not to improve one. Or we're tapped to redesign a site that may be visually unpleasing but isn't a complete failure.

How often are our skills put to the ultimate test? We see dozens of pages every day that need our care and attention, from top to bottom. How would we even know where to start?

With the following challenge, you won't choose what corner of the Internet needs improvement. It'll choose you.

> *"A picture is worth a thousand words. An interface is worth a thousand pictures."*
>
> —Ben Shneiderman

CHALLENGE

Execute the following instructions to the letter: 1) Turn on the radio. 2) Write down the third and fourth words within the first complete sentence you hear from the announcer or in a song. 3) Type those words into the Google search engine. 4) Hit the "I'm Feeling Lucky" button. 5) Redesign the user interface.

A good approach to this exercise would be to start with a rough inventory of all the content that is displayed on the page. Then, in sketch form, consider improvements to only the navigation. Move from the navigation to considerations of content organization: where material will appear on the page, via a sketched wireframe. After you've completed your wireframe, attack the visual design of your page and the discrete details of your information design and typography.

TAKE IT FURTHER

Move past the single page you've retooled and explore opportunities to improve the entire web site you've struck upon.

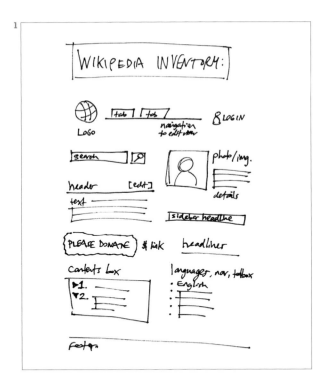

1

2

1,2,3 I was listening to my Pandora station and, per the rules of this challenge, randomly plucked the words "Tuesday's grey" from the song "Friday I'm in Love" by the Cure. Entering those words into Google and hitting "I'm Feeling Lucky" brought up the Wikipedia page for Danger Mouse's *The Grey Album*.

A good process to work through this challenge quickly is to do as I've noted here. First, draw on a sheet of paper all of the page elements divorced from the context of layout. Then, rank and prioritize those elements, deciding on a case-by-case basis what improvements can be made to each individual element. Then, bring those elements back together into a fairly tight sketch that expresses how they fit together as a coherent whole. Only then is it safe to jump into Photoshop or Illustrator and start rendering your improved user interface design. Otherwise, you'll end up solving a number of those problems while trying to polish the interface in the computer, which is very time consuming.

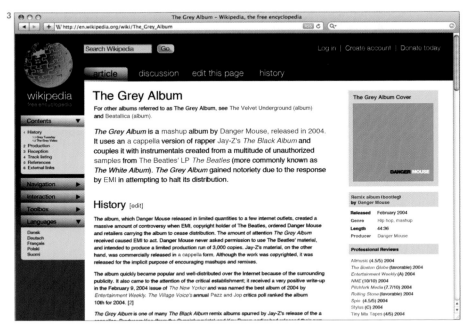

3

It Sounds Better on Vinyl

 90 minutes  Packaging

The compact disc may have radically transformed the fidelity with which we enjoy our favorite music, but if you've ever owned a record player, you know there is no substitute for kicking back and relaxing to the warm natural tones of your favorite songs. There's just something about vinyl that makes music feel more expansive.

LP record packaging was also bold. The visuals shout out for attention when you're leafing through the record crate. Now, there is no shortage of clever printing approaches for the compact disc, but the LP gives the designer more physical size for the cover—and designing for that scale inspires different possibilities. Big and bold visual ideas thrive at a larger physical scale—especially if they have a handmade feel. With this challenge, you'll get your chance to explore this medium.

> *"Record companies, in the early days, simply adapted the original vinyl sleeve design for the initial CDs and squeezed it unceremoniously into a two- or four-page booklet. Sacrilege!"*
>
> —Storm Thorgerson, *Mind Over Matter: The Images of Pink Floyd*

CHALLENGE

Tune the radio to your local variety or mix radio station. Write down the name of the first artist you recognize. You're now designing the LP cover of their latest greatest hits collection. In your design execution of the cover you must have a photograph that transitions into an illustration—or vice versa.

TAKE IT FURTHER

Design the back cover, sleeve and label that appears on the record. Then consider how it would look alongside other records from that recording artist's back catalog.

1 Inspired by the song "Tumbling Dice," Mark Notermann concocted a greatest hits album for the Rolling Stones' next release, *Boxcars*. Mark said, "In dice, double sixes is called 'boxcars.' It implies an abundance of material, trains, escape. It could have twelve songs, and even be broken in two sets of six like a vinyl LP."

2 Jessica Thrasher heard "Refugee" by Tom Petty and the Heartbreakers on the radio. Her design for their greatest hits LP incorporates hand-sketching and crumpled paper—deftly weaving references to several lyrics and themes from Petty's songs into her work.

3 Katharine Widdows's hand-drawn type puts the last thirty years of R.E.M.'s career to rest.

Storybook Ending

 30 minutes Book design, illustration, storyboarding

Once upon a time, there was a designer who wanted to create a children's book. She was an expert at drawing and painting in oils, but no matter how hard she tried, she couldn't come up with the right plot for the book of her dreams. This was a shame, because storytelling is a critical attribute of any piece of designed communications—and knowing how to write a meaningful story is a learned skill, not a nefarious talent.

For this challenge, hone your skills in storytelling and illustration for a youthful audience.

"As far as I'm concerned, all design is storytelling. Brochures and books tell stories in a very familiar way; they have covers, chapters and pages... even logos tell succinct moral tales. Thinking of design as an act of storytelling may help you focus your choices as you work."

—Christopher Simmons

CHALLENGE

Sketch out a ten- to twelve-panel storyboard for a book geared toward children ages three to seven. Organize your working process as follows to make your plot decisions more intuitive:

1. Spend ten minutes brainstorming an overall plot for the book. Summarize the arc of the story in a sentence.

2. Over the next ten minutes, come up with rough sketches of the visual direction and write some copy describing how the story would play out over twenty to twenty-four pages.

3. Use the rest of your time to tighten up your storyboards and tease out a moral, if you can.

TAKE IT FURTHER

Run your sketches by a toddler and read the copy out loud. Immediate reactions will be a good indication of the book's success or failure; toddlers are pretty honest folk. Is there anything you need to redo based on this feedback? Then, after you're done testing the material, consider making your book a reality by fully writing and illustrating it.

1,2,3 Over the course of thirty minutes, a team from one of my classes—Donnie Dinch, Meg Doyle, Claire Kohler and Mark Notermann—brainstormed the high-level concept for a children's book entitled *The Gloomy Galoshes*.

In the book, a girl named Toni has three pairs of shoes: sneakers, sandals and blue galoshes. Through the book, Toni's other shoes get taken out to the playground and the park. The galoshes grow sad, since they just sit in Toni's bedroom and wait to be worn. At the end of the book, there's a big rainstorm, and Toni takes her galoshes out to play. "The reward of being patient is sometimes great… a big messy jump in a puddle."

After the initial brainstorm, the team fleshed out full storyboards and copy for the book, then worked together collaboratively to illustrate it over the course of three weeks.

With sky this blue, sneakers are the perfect shoe for running and jumping and even standing still.

Princess?   Astronaut?   Pirate?

Its hard to tell who, Toni or her shoes, has the most fun while they run through the field. They seem to pull her along for a ride.

Splish!

Splash!

The reward of being patient is sometimes great.
Fun in the rain was well worth the wait!

4,5,6,7 The class took an iterative approach to the storyboard development, moving from very rough sketches of possible book illustration layouts to character studies that created a simple visual language that the entire team could share and execute for the final text.

21

Dead Philosphers Rock

 90 minutes　　 Book design

What is there to know about philosophy? The critical discourses of our time could fill dozens of hefty volumes and require many years of conscientious study to master their complexity.

One of the things I love about being a designer, however, is that we are often asked to find novel ways to reduce the appearance of complexity and make ideas more manageable for people to digest. You don't need a Ph.D. in Western philosophy to understand the essence of a series of ideas and express them succinctly to others. Though for the following challenge, that advanced degree wouldn't hurt.

"The charm of history and its enigmatic lesson consist in the fact that, from age to age, nothing changes and yet everything is completely different."

—Aldous Huxley

CHALLENGE

Come up with the overall look and feel for a series of short forty-eight-page or longer books that discuss key concepts provided by the most important philosophers of the ages: Aristotle and Socrates all the way up to Kant and Heidegger. As part of your solution, consider ways in which the books could be clustered or lined up on a shelf to create a larger visual motif with their narrow spines.

TAKE IT FURTHER

Translate your cover design concepts into an interactive timeline on the publisher's web site that explains the history of philosophy.

1,2,3,4,5 Dave Fletcher, creative director at theMechanism in New York City, took on this challenge. "I began the project by avoiding the obvious: beards. While one of my earliest ideas involved sketching all the philosophers and connecting them from 'beard to beard,' so to speak, in the end, I felt that the real solution to this particular problem would lie in categorizing and simplifying philosophic principals into digestible chunks. And it had to be modern and appealing."

Dave separated the book series into eight books that treat the "spectrum" of philosophic thinking throughout history: Aesthetics, Metaphysics, Mind, Epistemology, Language, Political, Ethics and Logic. He also thought about how the book experience could extend to the online space. "An expanded web component—only accessible by going to {book title}.deadphilosphers.com—would allow true buffs and/or masochists to dig deeper into the hearty details that await them."

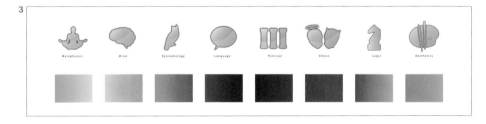

22

Opposites Attract

60 minutes   Book design

"Beauty is in the eye of the beholder," goes the old cliché. For designers, the opposite is often true. When you're solving a design problem, you often need to land on a beautiful *idea* for the appropriate audience before you start worrying about how good the idea will actually look in the final, designed execution.

So, what happens if you're asked to come up with a beautiful design idea about what beauty really means? What do you do when the entire foundation of your design is unnervingly objective, something that can be defined differently for each consumer? With this challenge, you're going to find out.

> **"When I am working on a problem, I never think about beauty. I only think about how to solve the problem. But when I have finished, if the solution is not beautiful, I know it is wrong."**
> —Buckminster Fuller

CHALLENGE

An editor at a major publishing house has contacted you and asked if you'll brainstorm cover concepts for an upcoming hard-cover book about perceptions of beauty throughout the ages. Ironically, the book is titled *Ugly* by author Jane Klingslaner. In the time limit provided, come up with a range of cover ideas, then select one of those ideas to draw out in a clean, professional comp that can easily be migrated into a computer execution.

TAKE IT FURTHER

Choose a specific style of execution that you must conform to before you begin your cover concepts. Will it be hand illustration, collage, photography or a type-only solution? Make a commitment to a specific medium or artistic method, and follow through on a set of executions.

1,2,3 "Am I so ugly that I need to put a paper bag over my face?" Yes, Mona, you are. During a twenty-minute individual brainstorm in one of my classes, Jessica Thrasher hatched this idea for the cover design of *Ugly*—proof that it doesn't take days of effort to yield a great concept.

4 In that same brainstorm, Michelle Cormack came up with the sketch of the following cover, which plays off the iconography of beauty pageantry.

# Book Report

 60 minutes ✳ Book design

Walking through a bookstore, it's easy to be inspired by great book covers by master designers like Chip Kidd and Barbara de Wilde. A well-considered book cover does more than put a pretty face on a work of literature—it embodies the metaphors and emotions submerged beneath the details of plot and character, grounding the book's overall theme. It must be compelling and informative within a limited space; a veritable wine label for literary complexity.

That's why the following challenge is so difficult!

 ## CHALLENGE

Pick up the phone, call a good friend and ask for a book recommendation. You'll need a one- to two-minute synopsis of the plot.

Now, you are the designer assigned to design the new paperback edition of said book. Can you create a meaningful book cover if you haven't read the book? You may not conduct any further research on your book other than reading the back cover and inside jacket flap.

"My hope is that when people first see the cover, they won't understand what they are seeing. Then, only as they read the book or the flap copy will that image change from dishes with dust on them to something else."

—Chip Kidd

TAKE IT FURTHER

Design a single chapter heading and the necessary front matter required to integrate your book cover design with the book's interior layout. Or, after you've finished your cover, read the book. Would you revise your design to match the book's content?

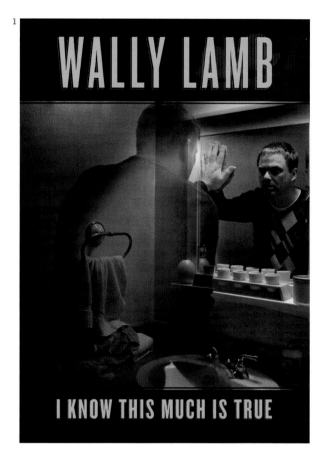

1,2,3 Mark Notermann was provided a summary from one of his classmates, Claire, for *I Know This Much Is True* by Wally Lamb: "Dominick is an identical twin whose brother, Thomas, is a paranoid schizophrenic. The book starts with Dominick's life at forty and alternates between the past and the present, so as a reader, you slowly find out more about the twins' unbelievably hard childhood, Dominick's ex-wife, the loss of their child in infancy, their abusive stepfather and repressed mother." Over a series of iterations, Mark settled upon the following cover concept/self-portrait that uncannily expresses the sense of duality that permeates the novel.

4 Another one of my classes took on a young-adult themed version of "Book Report." Michelle Cormack sketched this hand-drawn cover for *The Boy Who Cried Wolf and Other Tales* from *Aesop's Fables*—starting from a single paragraph from Wikipedia describing the content.

5 Katharine Widdows designed a cover for *Katie and Nan Go to Sea* by Nan Inger, which was recommended by Michelle, who said a good deal of the book "was filled with fishing, swimming and visiting friends in their summer homes. Sometimes the Dunkan misbehaved, as on the day when the smokestack caught fire; more often it was Katie and Nan who misbehaved; but then there were the really perfect times that the whole family would remember forever. The summer had to end, but Katie and Nan wished it never would." This was enough for Katharine to design a cover that captured the book's spirit.

He Shaves, She Shaves

 30 minutes  Packaging

Hair happens. And often in the places you wish it didn't grow. That's why there's shaving cream. Of all the various lotions, emollients, pastes and creams that clutter our bathroom counters, this magic substance has been around practically forever—thousands of years.

When shopping for shaving cream, it feels like the packaging design for this toiletry product hasn't progressed past 1983. Have you noticed the multitude of niche-targeted shaving creams? The aisles are jammed with cans advertising sensitive skin protection, mint-scented foam, extra hair-coating action, green-colored gel, citrus-infused non-lathering lotion. The list goes on forever.

Why isn't there a brand out there that makes it simpler to choose what shaving cream you should use? Try the following challenge and see if you can!

> *"Good design, at least part of the time, includes the criterion of being direct in relation to the problem at hand—not obscure, trendy or stylish. A new language, visual or verbal, must be couched in a language that is already understood."*
>
> —Ivan Chermayeff

CHALLENGE

Design packaging for a single type of shaving cream three ways: for women, for men and in a gender-neutral fashion. All three packaging ideas must be systematic, conveying via your design choices that they are a cohesive line of products.

In your brainstorming, feel free to choose a more sustainable option for your product's form than the normal aerosol dispenser.

TAKE IT FURTHER

Convey how your shaving cream concepts could be sold in a point-of-purchase display or on the shelf at the local drugstore. How could you have your product appeal to both men and women?

1 Are you BUFT? Jessica Thrasher brings a simple visual language to clearly convey masculine and feminine versions of the same product—as well as a gender-neutral, all-gray version.

2 The idea behind this shaving cream brand came from a name that Donnie Dinch brought into class—PheromoneMagnetic—accompanied by a sketch of a man and a woman icon attracting iron filings. Pictured is the dual-gender package, which is a marriage of the male and female editions.

3 Katharine Widdows created packaging with an elegant, Parisian feel for a brand of shaving paste scented with natural ingredients.

4 Mark Notermann brainstormed a clean and simple solution to this challenge: Men are from Mars, women are from Venus, and there's nothing more romantic than the full moon for either sex.

5 My quick solution to this challenge was to call my shaving cream Deface, complete with the anarchy symbol and yellow warning tape on the label. Punk rock shaving cream? Why not?

Totally Cereal

 30 minutes    Packaging

I can't imagine a complete morning without granola in my yogurt. Whether flakes, rolled oats or crunchy squares composed of twelve grains, most mornings begin with cereal—a product of American inventiveness. Most grocery stores devote a whole aisle to this multifarious product, and it's easy to be overwhelmed by the sheer variety of flavors.

But in many other cultures, cereal is a complete anomaly. Whether eating rice, fish, fermented beans or buttered tortillas, billions of people get along just fine without a bowl of Corn Flakes.

Which begs an important question: Just how important to our health are packaged cereals? Michael Pollan, writer and guru of responsible eating, says, "You're better off eating whole fresh foods rather than processed food products." And with the current trend toward eating whole unrefined grains and fewer sugars, abstaining from corn syrup, selecting products with organic ingredients and so forth, it's amazing to see just how many cereals continue to crowd the shelves while trumpeting health benefits that seem a little bit soggy.

Can you reinvent breakfast cereal for our health-obsessed times?

TAKE IT FURTHER

When you've settled on a packaging design direction that you like, sketch a flattened view that shows the layout of every panel on your box, bag or alternate cereal storage device.

CHALLENGE

Write one or two sentences describing a new type of breakfast cereal, including a brand name, audience, and type of store where this product will be sold. Your product idea must have at least one unique dietary feature that sets it apart from similar cereal products—e.g., organic ingredients, sustainably grown fruits, whole grains. Then, spend thirty minutes sketching at least two package design concepts for this new product.

"For while it used to be that food was all you could eat, today there are thousands of other edible foodlike substances in the supermarket. These novel products of food science often come in packages elaborately festooned with health claims... [but] if you're concerned about your health, you should probably avoid products that make health claims. Why? Because a health claim on a food product is a strong indication it's not really food, and food is what you want to eat."

—Michael Pollan, *In Defense of Food: An Eater's Manifesto*

100% ORGANIC INGREDIENTS

gran**olive**

pistachio
pumpkin seed
maple syrup
coconut
apricot
blueberry
sea salt

made with
100%
organic olive oil

Net Wt. 17oz 482g

1,2 I can't shake my addiction to breakfast cereal as part of my morning meal, so I've tackled this challenge a number of times to try to invent better alternatives to ordinary cereals. So far, the best solution I've created was GranOlive, a fictional brand of granola that's made with healthy olive oil and all-natural ingredients (modified from a great recipe that I'd seen in *The New York Times*). One afternoon, I tasked myself with creating packaging for GranOlive while I was cooking up a batch. I sketched packaging directions and logos while prepping ingredients, hopped onto the computer and rendered the package design while I was baking the granola—stopping every ten minutes to hand-turn the cereal browning away in the oven—and used the final product and leftover raw ingredients as part of my photographic rendering of the package. The photograph is all that's left of the afternoon; the granola vanished forthwith.

3 Designer Britta Burrus created the cereal Edible, "a low-carb, low-fat, high in fiber, certified organic, whole grain cereal—it is a tasty delight, morning, noon or night! This cereal brand uses only recycled materials for their packaging and searches out small, certified organic farms to provide their ingredients… The package is an 8" (20 cm) cube box; design is printed using two [PMS] colors while utilizing the box material as a color and texture. This design mix makes Edible stand out from the crowd, is easily stackable and helps emphasize the importance of recycling."

4 In one of my classes, we had two minutes to come up with a cereal description, then passed the description to the person across the table and sketched up two directions. This one was for Core, a healthier revision of Apple Jacks: "Naturally sweet, and won't destroy the roof of your mouth. Available in groceries everywhere."

Imaginary Film

 60 minutes   DVD cover, illustration, research

Action-packed typography. A bold ingénue enhanced by dramatic shadows conjured up by Photoshop. An atmosphere conveyed through color that hits you square in the gut.

Since you're in the trade of making pictures, you'll definitely enjoy this challenge.

CHALLENGE

Brainstorm a name and plot for a made-up film, including its genre and the decade in which it was produced. Using that description, create a DVD cover for the imaginary film that aesthetically conveys all of those details.

Will you be in the business of marketing a film noir pic made in 1980? A lost Woody Allen film from the '70s? Or the fourteenth sequel in a long-running line of horror classics? Seal in an envelope a one-sentence plot for your film. Then, show your DVD cover to some friends, ask them what they think it's about and open the envelope—just like the Oscars—to reveal if they're correct!

"As commercial art produced to sell another form of commercial art, film posters can often be crass, repetitive, disposable. They're just adverts to convince you to sit in a dark room for a couple of hours, right?... Well mostly, yes. But, as with the films themselves, amidst all the dreck you'll find the occasional poster that goes well beyond what is expected of it, a poster that deserves a life beyond the multiplex wall."

—Daniel Gray

TAKE IT FURTHER

If you're feeling especially bold, expand your DVD cover design into a full-size movie poster. Or, if you're stuck on your film's plot, choose one of your favorite films and reinterpret the original poster into a completely new graphic idiom.

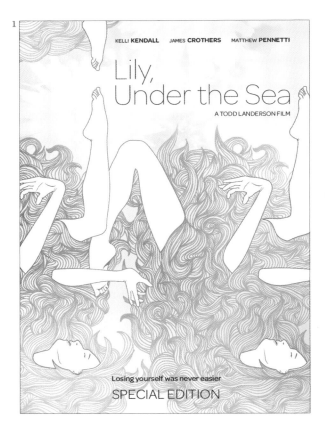

KELLI **KENDALL**   JAMES **CROTHERS**   MATTHEW **PENNETTI**

Lily,
Under the Sea

A TODD LANDERSON FILM

Losing yourself was never easier

SPECIAL EDITION

1 David Everly says that his imaginary film *Lily, Under the Sea* is "an offbeat comedy about Lily, a young twenty-three-year-old New York hairstylist struggling to make it on her own in the big city."

2 One of my classes agreed to design DVD covers for *The Last Steppe*, a historical drama from the 1970s. Jessica Thrasher created a cover with the following one-sentence plotline attached: "Chuluuny Bat is one of the remaining shamans of the Steppes people, struggling to survive and adapt to a changing Mongolia as Altan Khan proceeds to convert Mongols to Lamaist Buddhism in the late sixteenth century."

3 My take on *The Last Steppe* was to create a DVD cover for a movie included within the Criterion Collection. My plot was as follows: "A photographer whose mother recently passed away takes a long journey across the steppes of Mongolia—and through her art, rediscovers a part of her childhood that she had forgotten."

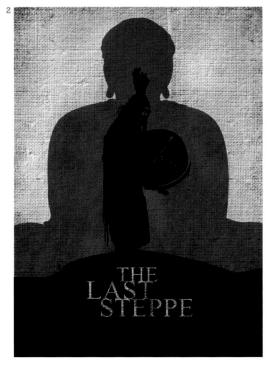

THE
LAST
STEPPE

the last steppe

A FILM BY JOE STREKASKY

1972   THE CRITERION COLLECTION

Creature Feature

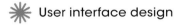

 60 minutes ✳ User interface design

There are an unlimited number of imaginary monsters that hold a cherished place in the horror movie pantheon: Godzilla, the Thing, Mothra, Frankenstein's monster, Dracula, the Wolf Man. Birthed from the minds of B-movie scriptwriters and then gobbled up like Milk Duds by an adoring populace, these films capture the still-beating bloody hearts of millions worldwide.

But if you're a layperson when it comes to creature features, how can you get up to speed with the latest and greatest gems of the genre and achieve fanboy status? With this challenge, you'll help create the next generation of horror movie aficionados.

"Listen to them— children of the night! What music they make!"

—Bela Lugosi in *Dracula*

CHALLENGE

Design the user interface for the homepage of a web site that highlights the history of monster movies. Besides the main site navigation, the homepage must feature the following: video clips from the most popular monster movies, the five most popular movies as noted by people that visit the site and a search function so you can explore the entire range of movies available. Be sure to sketch out a tight wireframe before you hit the computer.

While you're chewing on this challenge, think about the following: How would you tag and sort the movies within the web site? How do people rate the movies? What kind of community would you want to build around these movies? What kind of dialogue would you foster on the web site? How could you monetize this web site so you can make it self-sustaining?

TAKE IT FURTHER

Design an interactive experience as part of your web site's homepage that lets you choose a famous movie monster and have it destroy various cities around the world.

1

2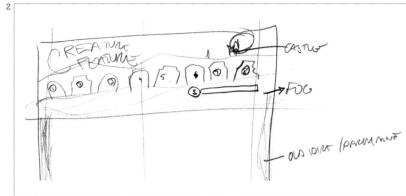

3

4

5

6

1,2,3,4,5,6 Designer and illustrator Nicholas Nawroth took the following approach in tackling this challenge: "I started out by doing some research on monster movies. I focused on classic monster movies because I love the posters from that era. From the beginning, I knew that I would base this project on those old movie posters. Alas, the more I tried to sketch out this project, the more it seemed like the ideas I was coming up weren't quite right."

Exercise 27

7,8,9 Nawroth continues, "The other issue was, what kinds of pages would the site have? I kept working on this project and putting it aside and finally had a breakthrough while sketching out my versions of the classic movie monsters: Frankenstein's monster, Dracula and the Mummy. After seeing these rough images, I realized my solution: The homepage would have a 'featured creature' and would be the most prominent image… On the real site, guest artists could render their favorite creatures in their own unique way.

"As for what pages the site would have, after much thought I narrowed them down to: Monster Media (artwork and videos of classic movies with ratings), Creature Guide (illustrated guide to every classic monster!), Forums and My Creature Lab (build your own creatures and save your favorite clips and artwork)."

# **28** **Ten-Second Film Festival**

 90 minutes   User interface design, information architecture

Online video is a deadly, addictive opiate for the design mind. It's also quite distracting. While I was attempting to write this paragraph, I was also reprioritizing my Netflix queue. My wife forwarded me some required viewing: two baby-elephant videos on YouTube. And later, I might get my Joss Whedon fix on Hulu…

Other than hosting great content, the web sites that I noted above are regularly optimized by designers for maximum throughput and ease of use. Designers continually work to reduce the amount of effort that users expend in accessing video content. Every detail of their interfaces has been methodically planned.

With the following challenge, discover what it's like to spend a day in the shoes of a user experience designer.

> *"I really have a very short attention span. I watch TV and think that commercials shouldn't be longer than ten seconds at the most."*
>
> —Barbara Kruger

 ## CHALLENGE

A client has approached you with an idea perfect for people with short attention spans: an online competition for the best ten-second videos created by independent filmmakers. Users can come to the web site and easily view, sort, select and vote (thumbs up or down) on any number of these short films. Create a user interface for the web site that fulfills this basic functionality, while also working to reduce the number of clicks required to view each brief film.

TAKE IT FURTHER

Would this same interface work if you made each movie only five seconds long? Two seconds? What would you need to change?

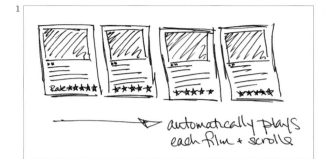

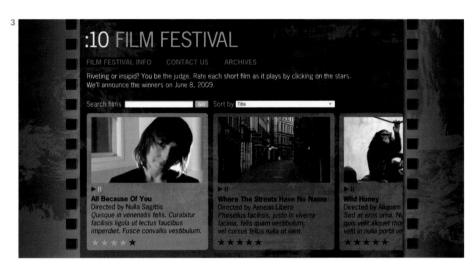

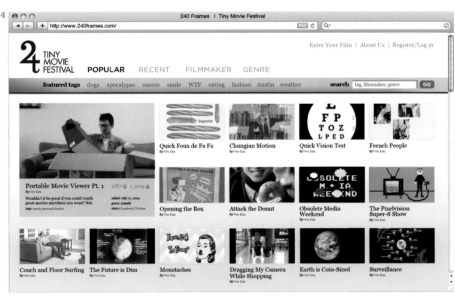

1,2,3 In graphic designer Grace Soto's initial design explorations, she wanted an energetic feel "appropriate to a web site showing motion pictures in very short bursts. The structure should be clean, clear and easy to navigate… [and] incorporate some sort of nod to old film reels." Because of the brevity of each movie, the web site would auto-play and scroll—a well-established design pattern that is often seen on Internet radio stations.

4 In my approach to this challenge, I wanted to take a common design pattern that you'd usually see on catalog web sites, only flattened onto one page. Upon loading the site for the 240 Frames Tiny Film Festival, the user would be presented with a gridded series of thumbnails. And when they clicked on any film thumbnail, the browser would swap in a video player that would stream and play the selected film then and there. You could then vote on the video, share it with a friend or move off that area to sample another video. A tag-based navigation would allow the user to search for movies of interest or click on exposed popular tags associated with topics of interest across the web site.

I've Got a Golden Ticket

 90 minutes Identity development, packaging, retail store experiences

When you step into a well-designed store where every element is arranged perfectly, it can feel like your eyes are dancing along to a bouncy jazz tune. You can find balance, rhythm and variety in spades. When designing for these types of retail experiences, setting the right pace for a customer is contingent on organizing and presenting a wide range of products coherently.

For this challenge, however, you'll be given a more limited palette.

"Simplicity is the ultimate sophistication."

—Leonardo da Vinci

CHALLENGE

Design a store experience for a chocolatier that sells only three types of chocolate: dark, milk and white. As part of your process, make recommendations regarding the naming and packaging of your product within the store, as well as for how you'll set up the space to convey an overall aesthetic.

Can you take a store that only has three products and make it come alive?

TAKE IT FURTHER

When you've completed your overall store concept, construct a physical prototype of your chocolate packaging system. What materials should you select to keep your chocolate fresh?

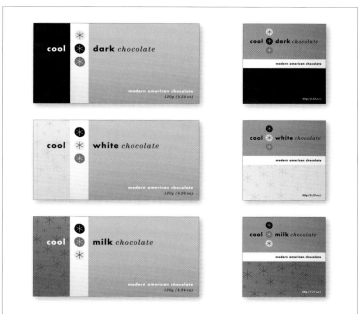

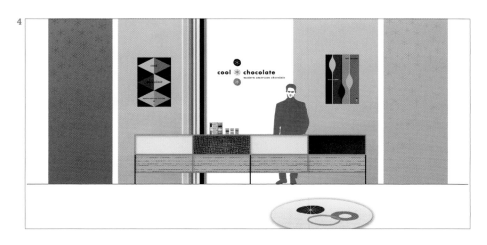

1,2,3,4 Jerry Lofquist, a designer in Los Angeles, decided to solve this challenge by creating a "legacy brand" that feels like it's been around for the past fifty years. Cool Chocolate's tagline sums it all up nicely: "Store in a cool, fertile place: 1950s California."

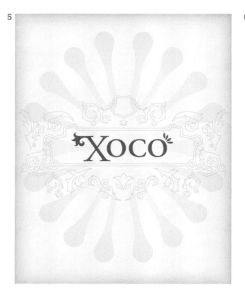

5

6

BEAKERS OF
SYRUP

POWDERS
PELLETS
PILLS
CHUNKS
MIXES

5,6 Mark Notermann created a logo for a store concept called Xoco, where chocolate alchemists (appropriately attired in lab coats) serve three types of chocolate from test tubes.

7 With this smart and sexy design, Donnie Dinch took the idea of three chocolate types and turned it into a brand called ChocoTrois. The chocolate bars for this brand would be packaged to look like double, queen and king-size beds—complete with rumpled sheets.

7

CHOCOTROIS

CHOCOTROIS

70% DARK FAIRTRADE KING

40% MILK FAIRTRADE QUEEN

Flapping in the Wind

 60 minutes  Guerilla advertising

What a sight to behold: As far as the eye can see, the sidewalk is littered with two-foot-tall ice cubes. A dog is trying to gain some sustenance by licking one of them. People are snapping pictures left and right. The whole plaza is starting to look like a circus. Then, as you walk closer, the impetus behind the stunt becomes as clear as water. They're trying to sell you iced coffee.

The furthest frontier of advertising is still what's known as the "guerilla campaign," where designers and writers create advertising concepts that exist in the physical world instead of in a television, on a laptop or in a magazine. Drawing from both the world of conceptual art and the invasive nature of a salesperson's patter, a well-executed guerilla stunt can burn an idea into a person's brain unlike any other advertising activity. And if filmed and disseminated into the working world, these stunts often become associated with the V-word—viral—thereby attaining millions of views on YouTube and the status of Holy Grail within the industry.

Take part in the following challenge and see if you can design an advertisement whose real-world manifestation is street theater.

> ## "As in all areas of advertising, substance *is more important than* form."
>
> —David Ogilvy, *Confessions of an Advertising Man*

CHALLENGE

Come up with a guerilla advertising campaign urging people to start drying their clothes outdoors whenever possible to save energy. The final deliverable would show what the tactic would look like in the real world, along with a description of how the experience would unfold.

While it would be nice if this were simply a public service announcement, the campaign is sponsored by a large Swedish home furnishings store to sell their new line of drying racks and clotheslines.

TAKE IT FURTHER

Write a blog post in the voice of someone happening upon your guerilla advertisement. Describe how she experiences the event from her perspective. Then, after writing the post, see if there are any ways that you could improve upon your original idea.

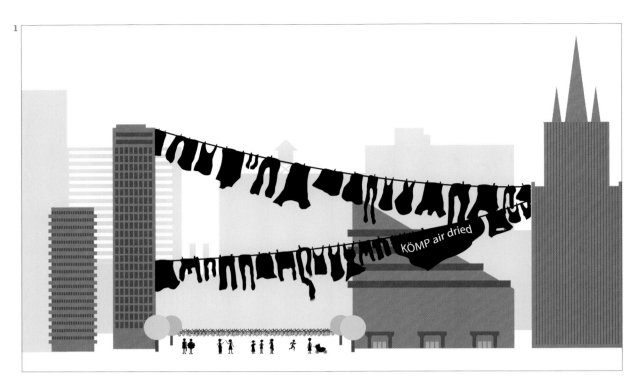

Check out our racks.

kant drying racks
25% off 'til July 31

KÖLN 1256 Norwegian Way
Richmond BC V6L 1T7
604-555-1212

1,2,3 In a thirty-minute class exercise, Michelle Cormack and Katherine Widdows brainstormed the following guerilla campaign for Kömp Air Dried.

As part of the promotion, giant laundry lines would be hung from downtown buildings and strung with a wide variety of clothing. Below the laundry, a gang of promoters dressed in T-shirts and boxer shorts would be out on the streets, handing out cards asking pedestrians to check out Kömp's "Kant" drying racks.

Going to Seed

 90 minutes User interface design, grid systems

I am a big proponent of eating local whenever possible. But when it comes to growing my own food locally, it would be fair to say that I have a brown thumb.

My backyard is a rock garden with evergreen shrubs. My balcony suffers from chill and rain at least ten months out of the year. During the other two, my poor plants take direct sun and high temperatures. Every crop I've attempted has perished, from simple basil and cilantro all the way to cucumbers and green peppers. Clearly, I need help from a professional or three. But I don't even know where to start…

In this challenge, create a community for those who lack the knowledge necessary to grow food in even the grittiest cities.

> ## "No two gardens are the same. No two days are the same in one garden."
> —Hugh Johnson

CHALLENGE

Create an online magazine in which failed city gardeners can receive the wisdom of top gardeners regarding urban horticulture and food preparation. Come up with a name for the magazine, design the masthead for its web site, and then set up an intelligent grid for the web site that will accommodate many different shapes and sizes of articles, recipes, reminiscences, photo essays and so forth.

One additional constraint: There must be a place independent of the magazine's regular content on each page that highlights a randomly selected plant—shown in seed form—to teach readers about the different kinds of plants they can grow in an urban environment.

TAKE IT FURTHER

After fully considering the details of the online experience, how would you translate your design into a print publication?

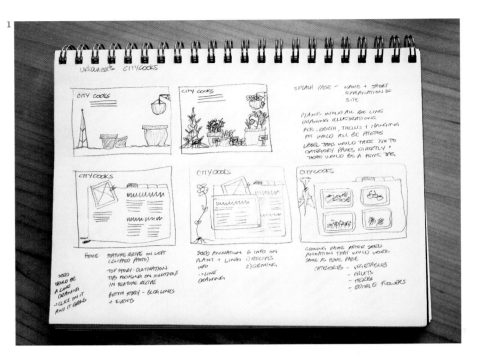

1,2 Michelle Cormack's CityCooks. com is organized by type of plant that you can grow in an urban setting: vegetable, fruit, herb or flower. In the homepage header, the plants shown would grow out of their pots and wind their way through the interface upon page load.

3 "Botanicity: Uniting city and country, so we can have it all." The homepage of Katharine Widdow's Botanicity.com prominently displays the six most recent articles, the required seed packet and also contains features centered around a city of the month. I'd love to see what culinary bounty is cultivated by urban gardeners in Paris…

Sell Me a Bridge

 60 minutes   Online advertising

Every state and province has its own quirky tourist destination that draws people from all over the world.

For example: Have you visited the Corn Palace? While driving through Mitchell, South Dakota, I was stunned into awed silence when I passed this monument. Used as a convention center, sports facility and paean to the fertility of South Dakota soil, the most unique features of the building were the intricate murals emblazoned across every wall—constructed entirely out of corn.

There's no way I would have flown to visit the Corn Palace from my home in Seattle if I'd seen advertisements regarding its wonders. It was sheer happenstance that our paths had crossed. How would a designer even begin to advertise visiting such quirky destinations, located in out-of-the-way towns?

With this challenge, you'll explore the various ways you can explain the virtues of traveling to one of these rare, yet rewarding locales.

TAKE IT FURTHER

If you're looking for an extra challenge, see if you can create a rich media ad or expanding banner that will immerse the user in exploring the actual place you've selected.

! CHALLENGE

Pick one of the following destinations: the Bonneville Salt Flats in Utah; the city of Saskatoon, Saskatchewan; Los Angeles County Department of Coroner; or the Corn Palace. In sixty minutes, come up with a compelling reason for people to visit your selected destination, then execute on your idea through online banner ad storyboards that artfully tell your story.

"Novelty has charms that our minds can hardly withstand."

—William Makepeace Thackeray

The Bonneville Salt Flats...

...more than you imagined.

1 In a thirty-minute brainstorm with Michelle Cormack, Jake Rae sketched out a rough storyboard for this banner advertisement for the Bonneville Salt Flats—home to everything from popular music videos to racecar drivers seeking a new land-speed record. Jake focused on the shimmering, almost alien landscape of the Flats to show that (almost) anything is possible on a visit there.

2 Starting with only a few frames of a brief and simple story usually works best in the medium of online advertising—and keeping your sketches intentionally crude at first won't get in the way of getting an idea on paper. It's what you do when you start making the idea—especially when working with technologies such as Flash—that cause all the heavy lifting. You'll want to think everything through on paper or a rough computer story-board before moving to animation, or the cost in time and effort to make changes will be quite painful.

Let's Take a Nap

 30 minutes   Posters

I'm sure you've heard the following adage: "Want it fast, good or cheap? Choose two out of three." The same rules don't apply to eating, sleeping and breathing. If you shortchange your nightly sleep—which is where our subconscious recovers from the day's travails—there's hell to pay in your design work.

When I sit down in my studio, I draw on my stores of experience in both my conscious and unconscious mind. If a design problem doesn't want to be solved, I often step away from my desk and take a stroll. By freeing up my logical mind, I create space for my subconscious to bubble up great ideas in the margins. And every night, sleep is the most productive time that the mind processes conscious experience. I can't count how many times an insoluble problem yielded an effortless result with a modest dab of shut-eye.

So, as a paean to this unsung muse of the working designer, take on the following sleep-inspired challenge.

TAKE IT FURTHER

Print out your poster at full size, put it up in the real world, then observe how people react to it as they walk past. Visually document their experience with a still camera or a video camera.

 CHALLENGE

Create a poster with the slogan: "Sleep: It's What You Need." In your execution, use an illustration style that is the antithesis of your usual artistic sensibility—i.e., if you gravitate toward simple, sans-serif typefaces, choose rough hand-drawn scribbles, and so forth.

> *"To achieve the impossible dream, try going to sleep."*
> —Joan Klempner

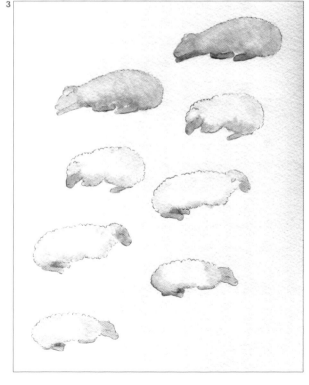

1,2,3 Just how many sheep have jumped over that fence? Cody Moore of Waking Illustration depicts what happens when you lose count and finally coast off to sleep. While solving this problem, she started with a series of ideas in sketch form, but quickly narrowed her focus to create this lovely hand-drawn execution.

Exercise 33

4,5 Katharine Widdows spotted a book pile at her local bookstore that looked comfortable enough to fall asleep on. This became the foundation of her design—and could easily lead to posters illustrating a range of places where tired souls fall asleep in public, such as in the produce aisle at the grocery store.

MATERIALITY

Can you feel it? You've got a face for type. Don't forget the postage. Tear up that poster design. Turn a logo into a magic trick. Make plaid fashionable again. With this branch from the backyard, I thee wed. Watch your brochure unfold, and unfold, and unfold. Say this three times fast: sticky-note zoo web site redesign. If you save up two thousand plastic bottles, you get a free couch. Custom-tailored stationery. Paper-bag puppets make great TV mascots.

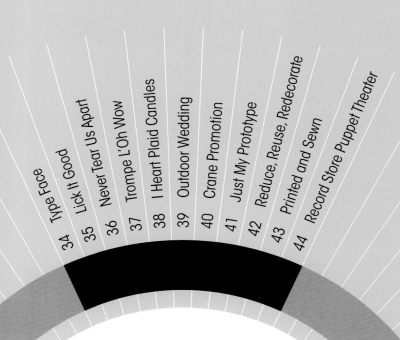

Type Face

 90 minutes   Illustration, posters, typography

Are those people on television really who they say they are? All too often, we reduce celebrities and politicians to sound bites, ingraining brief snatches from song lyrics, bold public speeches and tabloid headlines into the world's daily discourse.

From a journalist's point of view, selecting a memorable quote is a necessary activity that helps to tell a more powerful story. In the eyes of a designer, a well-known sound bite or quotation is charged with meaning in a different way. Well-known words exude a personality that pervades our public consciousness, suggesting both the speaker and the subject more so than any Twitter feed.

With this in mind, prepare to take on the following challenge about typecasting.

"I might repeat to myself, slowly and soothingly, a list of quotations beautiful from minds profound— if I can remember any of the damn things."

—Dorothy Parker

CHALLENGE

Find a personage of public renown whom you admire. Then, using hand-drawn or computer-set type, construct an illustration of this person's face using only text from words that he or she has spoken in public. See how you can best convey the spirit of the speaker through your sensitivity with type.

TAKE IT FURTHER

If you want an even greater challenge, consider illustrating the faces of a whole band using their lyrics, conveying actors in a scene from a famous movie, or recreating a historic event with multiple people.

1 Mark Notermann hand-sketched his type face from quotes by President Barack Obama.

2 Jake Rae built his type face from a famous quote by Bill Cosby: "In order to succeed, your desire for success should be greater than your fear of failure."

3 From free-form and flowing script, Jessica Thrasher constructed with type a classic portrait of Albert Einstein during one of his sillier moments.

Lick It Good

 🕐 90 minutes   ✳ Illustration, paper engineering

Waiting in line at the post office, I couldn't help but notice the vast intricacy inherent in a bold display of stamps. From the art of Disney to a new series meant to look like vintage movie posters, the amount of detail finessed into each illustration was remarkable.

As designers, we're more used to working with large-scale press sheets or low-fidelity pixels on a screen than a few centimeters of glue-smeared paper. The necessary attention to small-scale detail is what makes this next challenge so difficult.

> *"Sometimes the simplest solutions are literally just staring you in the face. The issue of designing stamps is really that you gaze at designs on your screen, all the time forgetting quite how small they end up. When designing stamps you spend most of your time taking things out, not putting them in."*

—Michael Johnson

TAKE IT FURTHER

Envision and design a commemorative booklet that would enclose your stamps. Look to stamp sheets online, a stamp collecting shop or your local post office for further inspiration.

CHALLENGE

You've been asked by your country's post office to design a series of six commemorative postage stamps that celebrate energy conservation. For your stamp designs, choose an illustration style from one of the following types:

Collage: All elements cobbled together from found images and text.

Stippled: Illustrations comprised entirely of pinpoint dots that form specific shapes.

Gouache or pastel: Work with an artistic medium that relies on softness of line for its effect.

Photo-realistic: Use photography and live digital type as the foundation of your design.

Folk art: The design is comprised of colored and patterned paper shaped into form and type.

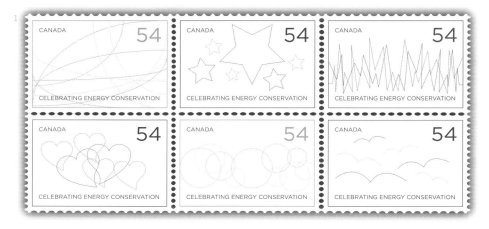

1 Michelle Cormack worked from the "stippled" illustration style, creating six Canadian stamps whose iconography was evoked by colored dots on a white background.

2 With "collage" as his medium, Jake Rae designed a set of iconic stamps that mixes photography, illustration and type in playful ways.

3 Katharine Widdows was assigned "folk art" as her illustration style for this exercise. Her stamp designs display a playful whimsy that holds up well when viewed at a tiny size.

Never Tear Us Apart

 60 minutes   Posters

There's definitely a specific style that accompanies music poster design: sleek Illustrator art touched up with a bit of grit, merged with hand-drawn type that precisely fits into well-defined shapes. Then, when the posters are screen-printed, the designer gets inventive regarding what order the inks hit the paper to create unique interactions between colors. Stick twenty of those creations up at local record stores, give a few to the band and put the rest online for your fans to buy at $20.99 (plus shipping and handling).

Now, don't get me wrong. I love this style of poster design, and especially the work of the Small Stakes and Patent Pending Industries. But I also like to see how designers can think outside the trappings of this most artistic medium.

So, for the following music poster challenge, let's see how you can tear things up. Literally.

CHALLENGE

Create a poster for a rock concert in your neighborhood. Instead of planning and executing your design via pencil or computer, make the poster completely out of torn things: pieces of paper, solid objects, found elements and collage.

Once you've solidified your layout, photograph or scan the resulting poster, bring it into a photo-editing program and begin to play with how it will be reproduced to advertise the upcoming gig.

TAKE IT FURTHER

Sketch out how the artistic motifs used in your poster could be used to decorate the stage at the show.

"By all means break the rules, and break them beautifully, deliberately and well. That is one of the ends for which they exist."

—Robert Bringhurst

Exercise 36

1,2,3,4,5,6 "Twistie Ties make nice type!" Designer Jarred Elrod created this poster for a compelling Tennessee-based band called Tenderhooks. After mocking up the design as a collage with various torn elements assembled from elements he'd stored up in his home, he scanned the appropriate graphic elements into his computer piece by piece and converted it into printable four-color art.

7 Trompe L'Oh Wow

 90 minutes   ✳ Identity development

I think every child goes through a phase where he's obsessed with magic. From the large-scale illusions of David Copperfield all the way down to the local magic-shop owner palming coins before a crowd of two adoring twelve-year-olds, the practice of magic is a wide-eyed delight for millions—and an exclusive club for those who choose to explore its secrets.

Designers can be magicians as well. The FedEx logo immediately comes to mind, with its witty placement of an arrow within the mark. With just a pencil and paper, we can conjure up similarly surprising illusions that bend our perceptions of space and time. But no matter what methods you choose to employ, your visual trickery must be simple enough to disguise with a little sleight of hand—and smart enough to metaphorically act as a representative of the whole. After all, the most effective illusions are those whose expressions vanish softly into the fabric of a well-formed idea.

In this challenge, you'll get a chance to practice your craft on the one audience that will most appreciate your efforts.

"What the eyes see and the ears hear, the mind believes."

—Harry Houdini

! CHALLENGE

Create a logo for the Global Magic Society, a national invitation-only group of upper-echelon magicians. As part of your design exercise, you must incorporate an optical illusion into your mark.

TAKE IT FURTHER

Create a brand kit that explains the new identity to Global Magic Society members. But when opening the kit, the logo must be revealed in a manner that's a trick in and of itself.

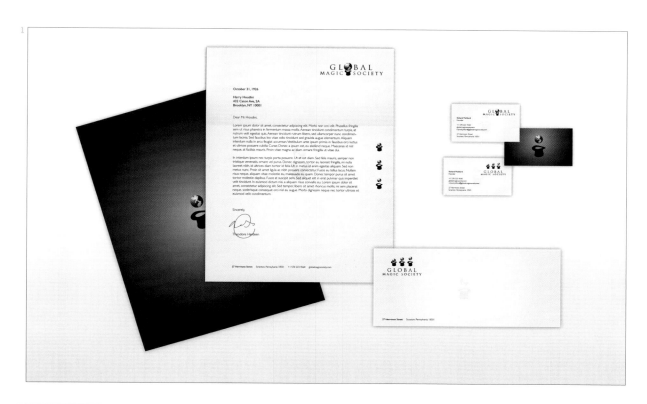

1,2,3 The following logo magic is courtesy of Dave Fletcher, creative director at theMechanism in New York City. "I'm a fan of presenting multiple uses of a logo when appropriate… The idea is to use the word 'global' along with traditional magician props—in this case, the hat, the rabbit and the dove. Instead of a magician pulling the rabbit out of the hat, the shapes—the rabbit being pulled out of the hat by the dove—all nicely fit into continental shapes to create a bit of an optical illusion or trickery for someone who looks closer."

For the stationery package, Dave's idea was "to print on slightly translucent paper. The use of the paper for the envelope, letterhead and business card serves several purposes… When folded, the back of the letterhead displays the logo in the center—the translucency of the envelope allows the logo to show through slightly, creating a really nice watermarking effect. There are three possible uses of the logo, all achieving the same effect."

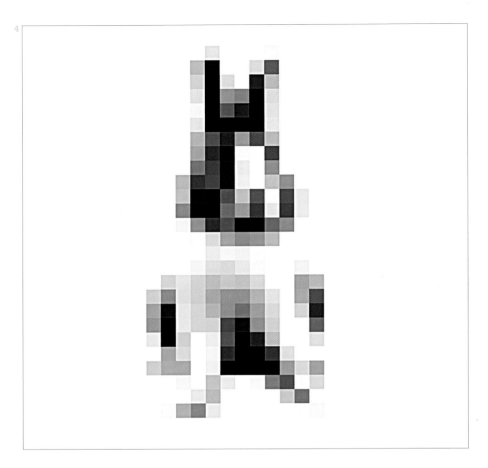

4 In Dave's initial explorations, he played with "the idea of bitmapping a familiar magician prop until it was unrecognizable—forcing the audience to squint to see what it is. (Much as they might do while watching a magician and trying to figure out the trick.)"

5 Lawrence Miller, an editor and designer at Pennsylvania State University, conjured up this logo that is equal parts Bauhaus and typographic trickery.

I Heart Plaid Candles

 120 minutes    Packaging, identity development

Designers use a wide variety of patterns in their work to create variety, dimension and feeling in what could otherwise be a flat, empty execution. And there's no pattern that's more ubiquitous than plaid.

Start with the illustrious tartan. Over the past few hundred years, these kilts woven in bold plaid patterns transitioned from regional style to clan identifier to a design pattern that says Scotland—no matter whether it's emblazoned across a beach blanket, a pair of sunglasses or the wall of your hotel room. Then there's madras plaid. Argyle. There's quite a list of fabric styles derived from this funky weave of varicolored threads.

As designers, knowing what pattern to choose as part of your design—and what feeling that pattern conveys, from luxury product to Blue Light Special—only comes with practice. Use the following challenge to exercise your pattern-selection skills.

> *"Creativity involves breaking out of established patterns in order to look at things in a different way."*
> —Edward de Bono

CHALLENGE

Create the name, identity and overall packaging concept for a new luxury brand of soy-based candles whose overriding graphical motif is the use of bold plaid patterns. As part of your explorations, you'll need to home in on what attributes of color, texture, and form best convey your product's sensibility.

TAKE IT FURTHER

Design an advertisement that announces the release of your new line of candles. Or, if you're looking for an even bigger challenge, determine how you could extend your line of candles to include paisley patterns as well.

1,2 Jessica Thrasher created this sleek, stylized interpretation of the argyle plaid pattern for her line of soy candles. Each of them comes in a metal tin that can be refilled with new candles after the previous one has been depleted.

3 Jake Rae's candle brand, Humdinger Candle Co., has a light Christmas-like feel that says, "Great holiday gift."

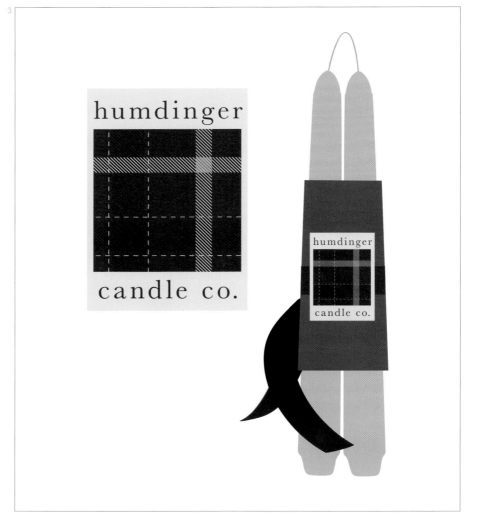

Outdoor Wedding

 60 minutes Collateral, paper engineering

Whether we're using the golden mean as the basis of a layout, or employing natural-world motifs and patterns as textures throughout a design, we spend a great deal of time within the computer finessing lines and shapes into pleasing organic forms. Much as we choose to bring plants into the grittiest urban locales to soften an otherwise harsh man-made environment, we make design choices that are reflections of our natural world. And right outside our window, we're surrounded by an infinite variety of those same organic forms, providing endless inspiration.

In this challenge, you'll be required to step away from your computer and physically bring the untamed world into your design work.

"Shall I not have intelligence with the earth? Am I not partly leaves and vegetable mould myself?"

—Henry David Thoreau

CHALLENGE

Go out into your yard or a local park and collect twigs, leaves and bark that suggest design possibilities. (From the ground, not from living trees—your neighbors may not like you plucking their petunias.) Then, once you're back in your studio, use the leaves and twigs you found to craft a beautiful handmade wedding invitation concept for the future Marty and Laura Longerman. You can choose the place and time.

One critical factor in your design: Your concept for the card, when printed, must accommodate a different piece of unique plant matter for each guest.

TAKE IT FURTHER

How could you effectively produce 250 of these cards? What resources would be required to complete the cards in twelve hours? In eight hours? What would you need to rethink about your card design in order to make it happen?

1,2,3,4,5,6,7,8 A brief walk outside yielded more than enough material necessary for this gorgeous wedding invitation by Cody Moore of the Missouri-based studio Waking Illustration. The intelligent use of white space in her design can accommodate a wide variety of different flower and leaf arrangements… although the level of time investment required for sewing the plant matter into place on an invitation-by-invitation basis would require many weeks of conscientious effort to produce a few dozen.

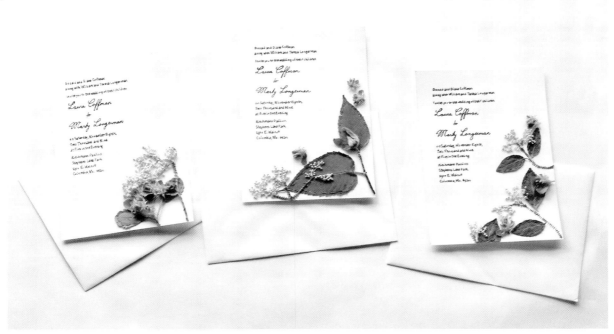

Crane Promotion

 90 minutes Collateral, paper engineering

The flat sheet of blank paper beckons to you, full of creative possibilities. In deft hands, will it become a crane, a fox, a boat or a box?

Those who have mastered print design know that when they approach the creation of a collateral piece, they should think not only about what will be printed on the page, but also how the reader's experience of the content will unfold over time. In a designer's hands, the fully printed page is yet another element that can be manipulated for artistic effect.

With this challenge, be ready to explore the myriad ways that a sheet of paper can reveal a compelling message.

> **"I think I did pretty well, considering I started out with nothing but a bunch of blank paper."**
> —Steve Martin

CHALLENGE

You've been tasked by the International Origami Society to create a brochure promoting the value of membership in their organization. Through illustration, type, color use and your paper engineering skills, tell a story about the value of origami as an international pastime.

In order to demonstrate the joys of recreational paper folding, the brochure must utilize at least seven unique folds in its construction.

TAKE IT FURTHER

Design two brochures for an upcoming class taught by visiting origami masters. They must interlock in a visually pleasing fashion as part of a table display at your local Origami Center.

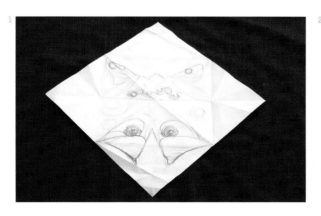

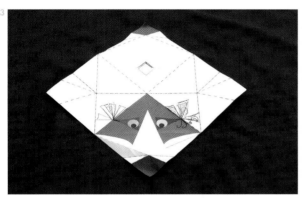

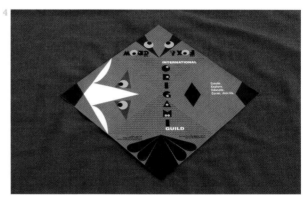

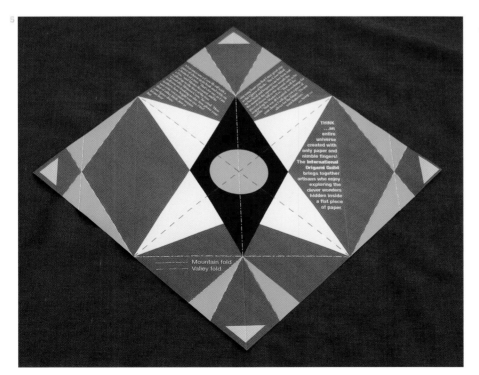

1,2,3,4,5,6,7,8,9,10,11

"Think… an entire universe created with only paper and nimble fingers!" reads the copy in designer Melanie Gilliam's solution for this challenge. And the reader of this brochure can use his nimble fingers to transform her brochure into either a fox or a crow. "I was lucky to find that Aesop wrote a fable about a fox and crow and added it to the brochure. Of course my brain lit up like a roman candle and I started to think of all kinds of other possibilities for subsequent brochures…"

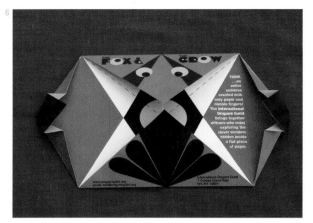

6

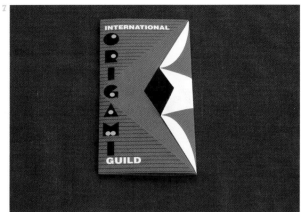

7

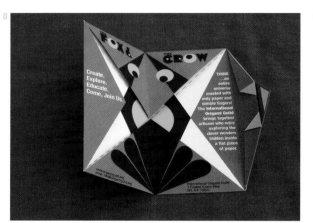

8

9

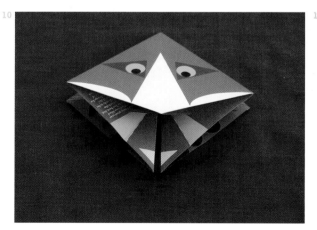

10

11

Exercise 40

Just My Prototype

 120 minutes　　 User interface design

I adore my local zoo. Their exhibits are designed as free-ranging spaces for animals from different habitats to commingle. When taking friends or children there, it feels more like a safari through the savannah than a visit to an animal preserve.

And speaking of safaris—try to visit their web site. Talk about a brutal excursion that bears no resemblance to your real-world zoo visit. Their homepage is crammed full of incongruent links. There's no global search, no exposed navigation on secondary pages, no grid or coherent structure underlying the information design. It makes you want to take out your machete and hack away the interface until some semblance of order emerges.

In the following challenge, you'll get to strap on your pith helmet and embark on a roaring-good web site redesign.

"Web design is not book design, it is not poster design, it is not illustration, and the highest achievements of those disciplines are not what web design aims for. Web design is the creation of digital environments that facilitate and encourage human activity; reflect or adapt to individual voices and content; and change gracefully over time while always retaining their identity."

—Khoi Vinh

CHALLENGE

You've been asked to create an improved user interface for your local zoo's web site. Begin your journey by sketching out ways that you can improve the navigation, the overall page grid, the visual presentation and arrangement of content, the possible addition of social networking features and so forth.

But before you hop onto the computer and start pushing pixels, create a paper prototype of your interface using pieces of paper, scissors, glue and a marker. Then put your ideas in front of another person and have him pretend to use your design, describing what he'd expect to see as he "clicks" on the various buttons and other links.

Based on his input, revise your design concept as necessary—then execute in the computer, if you wish.

TAKE IT FURTHER

Think through the in-depth details associated with any interaction: rollovers for buttons and navigation, tool tips, opening and closing drawers or accordion menus, and any areas that may have enhanced interactivity through use of existing web technologies.

1,2,3 In a class exercise, Mark Notermann was given an old screen design (1) for the Woodland Park Zoo in Seattle. Mark took this design and rethought its overall information architecture and user interface through the construction of a simple paper prototype (2). He then used this paper wireframe as the foundation for a clean, sophisticated redesign of their entire web site (3). "To make a more engaging online experience for visitors to the zoo's web site, video was put on the homepage. A news feed and blog feeds are also available with limited previewing via accordion menus. It also features a cleaner interface with a friendlier color scheme, and all the necessary information is easily accessible from an intuitive two-layered menu."

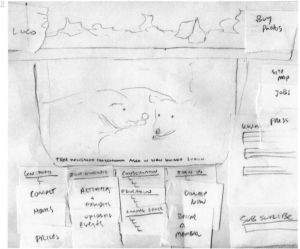

Reduce, Reuse, Redecorate

 120 minutes Product design, paper engineering, physical prototyping

My vision of future fashion, when it comes to home furnishings, is the concept of reuse.

We can no longer choose to make products out of plastic and expect them to magically vanish off the face of the planet when they reach the ends of their use. We need to understand how to reuse the materials surrounding us, not just recycle used materials into the same forms until they entirely degrade. Otherwise, we'll never be able to reduce the number of products that already choke our landfills and overtake the Pacific Ocean.

I'm all for the craft revolution brought upon us by the *ReadyMade* magazines of the world—and we have the capacity as designers to imagine truly inspired designs that, if primed for mass production, take care of our trash instead of creating more of it.

With this challenge, you'll get a chance to design furniture that does just that.

TAKE IT FURTHER

Show how your creation would be featured on a web site like Etsy, including descriptive copy and price.

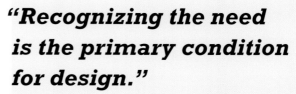

> "Recognizing the need is the primary condition for design."
> —Charles Eames

CHALLENGE

Take a recyclable object that we purchase regularly when going about our everyday lives—bottles, cans, cutlery, plates, cups, magazines, whatever works—and design a piece of furniture that uses it in multiples.

As part of your planning process, consider if your furniture would require detailed instructions for construction or would be delivered in an entirely constructed state.

1 One of the big inspirations for this challenge was the ReVision project from Artists for Humanity, a Boston nonprofit that provides urban youth with the keys to self-sufficiency through paid employment in the arts. The ReVision tables are recreated from reclaimed junk mail and magazines. Once the pieces are assembled, the surfaces are finished with a no-VOC eco-friendly resin, which is water resistant and easy to clean with eco-friendly products.

2,3,4 Another inspiration for this challenge was the "Meltdown" series by Tom Price, a furniture and product designer established in London. "These chairs are part of a series commissioned by Arts Co. for the exhibition 'From Now to Eternity,' and are made exclusively from discarded polyester fleece clothing. The seat area is created by placing layers of clothing onto a hot steel seat-shaped former. As it heats, the fabric begins to melt, exposing and integrating colors and patterns of the various layers. When cooled, the surface is transformed into a rigid, shiny, colorful display."

Printed and Sewn

 90 minutes Identity development, paper engineering

How many Pantone colors did you use on that business card? Was it embossed? Did you apply a foil stamp or die-cut the corners? When creating an identity system, we often focus on the most effective and efficient ways to mechanically reproduce our designs, debating the merits of printing on a Heidelberg press versus a Komori press, rather than pushing ourselves into more intimate methods of production.

For this challenge, can you think outside the printing press and grow comfortable designing with a needle and thread?

"Fashion is not something that exists in dresses only. Fashion is in the sky, in the street, fashion has to do with ideas, the way we live, what is happening."

—Coco Chanel

CHALLENGE

You've been asked by a local fashion designer to create her stationery system. This designer specializes in stitching her own patterns over vintage clothes found at estate sales. In your stationery materials, you must incorporate hand- or machine-stitched thread.

It may be time-intensive to produce your idea, so you might need to consider ways in which you could manufacture your sewn designs in a cost- and time-effective manner.

TAKE IT FURTHER

Could you extend your sewn motifs into other branded elements, such as store signage, collateral or a web site?

1,2 Say hello to Marguerite Choufleur, sole proprietor of Deco-Rational Apparel Design. This card design is the brainchild of creative director Carrie Byrne, who felt a great way to solve this challenge would be to have her Punxsutawney, Pennsylvania-based designer sew snaps into the card itself.

3 One of the inspirations for this exercise came from this business card by apparel and graphic designer Ethan Martin. As part of his card design, Ethan hand-painted the cards with watercolor, then sewed his contact information onto the card with red thread.

Record Store Puppet Theater

 60 minutes Identity development, retail store experiences, hand animation

Did you see the commercial where the cars flew through the air, transformed into robot animals and blew up London?

Watching television nowadays, commercials feel like big Hollywood productions pumped full of slick CG effects—and entirely lacking in the human touch. Wouldn't it be nice for a client to come along and solicit a television ad that depended on scissors and glue instead of bright-smiling actors and digital manipulation?

In the following challenge, you'll shoot your own TV spot—but instead of fancy post-production and famous actors, the stars of your commercial will be puppets.

"There's just something visceral about moving a puppet frame by frame. There's a magical quality about it. Maybe you can get smoother animation with computers, but there's a dimension and emotional quality to this kind of animation…"

—Tim Burton

CHALLENGE

Come up with the name and logo for a "record store of the future" where people can purchase physical CDs and DVDs, then have digital files of the songs and movies wirelessly auto-downloaded to their mobile devices. This logo and name will be used in the end-frame of your commercial.

Then, sketch up storyboards and a script for a thirty-second television spot advertising the grand opening of your store. The entire ad concept must be shot in one take, and your storyboards must incorporate handmade puppets and materials.

When your ad concept comes together on paper, use a video-recording device such as a digital camera, video camera, Flip Mino, camera phone, etc., to create your ad. Every second of your spot must be caught on film—no effects or editing in post!

TAKE IT FURTHER

Your first ad was such a hit that your client wants to bring your puppet characters onto their record store's web site. Record a set of short videos that can be used to highlight special offers.

1 For this challenge, Seattle-based designer Scott Scheff and I created a thirty-second commercial within a thirty-minute time frame on a Flip Mino camcorder. In the commercial, our puppet hero is listening to the Pixies's "Wave of Mutilation" while huffing Elmer's (nontoxic) glue. Inevitably, he gets so excited that he starts eating the stuff. The camera pans away to the end card, thereby saving us from the aftermath of the puppet's drug binge. Designer Mark Notermann devised in ten minutes the name and logo for our record store: Un1fi.

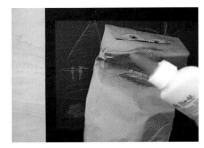

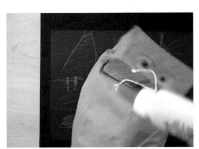

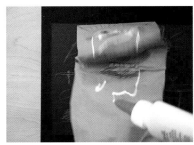

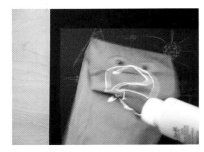

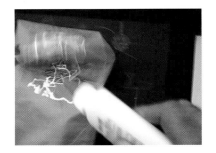

Exercise 44

INSTRUCTION

Time to follow directions. Prepare your robot army for world domination. Let someone make that poster for you. Making pasta, then telling the tale. Thanks, I'll check out my own groceries. Sustainability at play.

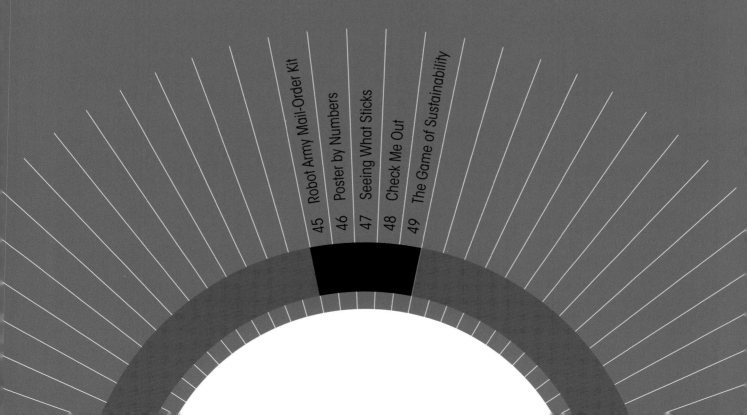

Robot Army
Mail-Order Kit

🕐 60 minutes ✳ Information design, paper engineering

In the back of a comic book, tiny black-and-white ads beckon to you with their mysterious treasures. Will you send away for a model rocket that you can launch in your backyard? Perhaps you could use a decoder ring to help you trade messages with your best friend in math class. Or would you like a set of plans for constructing your very own robot? Just send us $8.95 plus $4.95 shipping and handling.

Since you're a designer, you don't need to buy the plans for making a robot. You can design one on your own. And in the process, you can glean some insight into the realm of paper engineering—where you must not only become adept at learning how to shape flat substrates into a variety of forms, but also be able to externalize your design vision into a tangible list of steps that clearly conveys how to bring your idea to life.

> ### CHALLENGE
>
> Draw up easy-to-follow plans to construct a robot of your own design out of various household materials: paper, pipe cleaners, buttons, cardboard tubes, etc. Give the plans and materials to a friend, then watch and take notes as she builds what you've designed. The robot must be able to be built in ten minutes or less.

TAKE IT FURTHER

Create a more elaborate, collectible robot that can be constructed, personalized and decorated by its owner. Then take a series of photographs showing your robot terrorizing the populace.

"If popular culture has taught us anything, it is that someday mankind must face and destroy the growing robot menace."

—Daniel H. Wilson, *How to Survive a Robot Uprising*

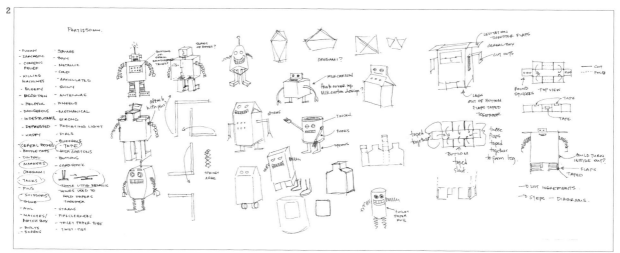

Robot Army Mail-Order Kit

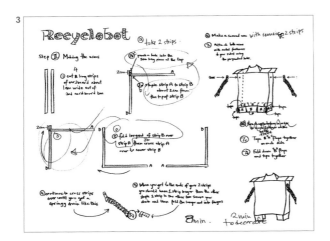

1,2,3,4,5 For this challenge, designer Grace Cheong wanted to make sure her final robot design (1) was possible to build in five minutes flat. She handed out the materials and the instructions (5) to assemble her robot to a series of test subjects (4), and from their response she reduced the number of steps necessary to create her robot and meet her time constraint.

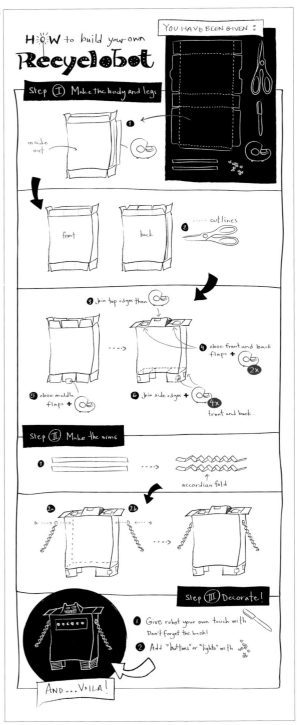

Exercise 45

Poster by Numbers

 60 minutes   Posters

"The layout doesn't feel cohesive yet." "Are you sure a green-to-white gradient is the right treatment for that background?" "I thought the client wanted seven-year-old children's photos on the cover." "The headline isn't kerned." "Have you tried a serif typeface for the body copy?" "After you've addressed these changes, can I see the revised comps before the end of today?"

If you've ever worked in a design studio or creative agency, you've probably had an art director boss you around. This isn't a bad thing. Art directors help guide designers toward stronger, on-brief creative solutions. We're often too close to the work to see what they see. And it takes years of concentrated design effort to gain the vocabulary necessary to help direct projects well.

Want to feel what it's like to be an art director? Try the following challenge to find out.

> *"Education is the period during which you are being instructed by somebody you do not know, about something you do not want to know."*
>
> —G.K. Chesterton

CHALLENGE

Select an AIDS prevention charity that you'd like to support. Write a detailed list of instructions—along with a creative brief, if you so desire— for creating a poster that will urge onlookers to donate money to said charity. Then provide your instructions to a non-designer and see what he creates. You may not pre-design or render any portion of the poster as a reference aid in the instructions.

The results you receive from this exercise will entirely depend on the level of specificity you provide. You can experiment by leaving key details open-ended, such as photography, illustration, typography and content, and see what happens.

TAKE IT FURTHER

Provide creative feedback to your designer after he has provided you with his first round of comps and guide him through a round of design revisions.

Instructions

This assignment is to create a poster soliciting support for AIDS prevention.

1. Find an image in print of a microphone. The classic, round-ended, phallic microphone most commonly used. The best place I can suggest to find this would be Guitar Center—they have catalogues you could take. Radio Shack might also have something like this. You could also directly photocopy a real one if you have one handy. I have one you could use.

2. Get a banana. Remove any stickers that are on it. Peel it halfway and eat the exposed half of the fruit. Take it to a photocopy machine and copy it directly. Try to arrange the skin pieces in a lovely way if possible.

3. Find an 11" x 17" (28cm x 43cm) sheet of white paper.

4. Cut out the microphone with scissors.

5. Cut out the banana image with scissors.

6. Remove the banana fruit and put the microphone in its place. If the sizes seem unmatched, use photocopiers to adjust this. I'd like the entire image to be large on the poster, but you will need room on the top and bottom for text.

7. Position the microphone-banana down on the sheet in the center.

8. The main (largest) text on the poster will be "This willie doesn't need a love glove." Place it above the image. You can hand-draw block letters or cut out type from magazines and newspapers to create this phrase. (If you want to write this on a separate sheet and then cut and glue it onto the poster, that might help to keep things movable and to fit everything on.)

9. Underneath the image add the following phrases, handwritten legibly, centered if possible:

   (medium-sized type) "Don't keep AIDS prevention under wraps."

   (below medium type, small-sized type) "The Global Media AIDS Initiative (GMAI) highlights best practices in relevant, accurate and effective HIV/AIDS programming from campaigns around the world. Creative talent and technical resources are put to work to produce public service ads (PSAs) and integrating powerful HIV/AIDS themes into news, public affairs and entertainment programming. Precious airtime and advertising space is then used to disseminate HIV awareness and prevention messages in some of the hardest-hit countries and regions of the world. Until there's a cure, education is our best defense against this ruthless, quickly spreading epidemic. Support the GMAI today by visiting www.thegmai.org."

10. Now that everything is placed, glue all the elements down on the poster.

11. You're almost done. Photocopy the poster once on white 11" x 17" (28cm x 43cm) paper. You can pick the color. Feel free to play with contrast and any other image settings on the machine to get interesting effects.

12. Feel free to hand-color parts of the poster if you want—the text, parts of the image, or whatever, you can decide. Use crayons, markers or whatever's handy.

13. Call me when you're done and I will come pick it up. Hope that was easy enough and you had fun! And thank you; I owe you a drink or two.

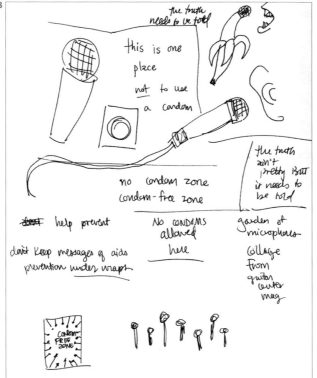

1,2,3 Katherine Widdows wrote up instructions (1), then provided them to Melanie Noel, who followed them to design this poster (2). You can see the development of the project in the her sketches (3).

 # Seeing What Sticks

 60 minutes   Interaction storyboarding

"How do you make spaghetti?"

This was a question posed by design professor Mark Baskinger's seven-year-old daughter. "In trying to explain all of the steps to her, I struggled to remember what I would do first. Do I open the cabinet and decide which kind of pasta I'll make? Or do I first start the water boiling with a dash of salt? And at what point do I start the sauce for a slow simmer on the stove? In an effort to answer her question thoughtfully—and to avoid patronizing her with a response such as, 'Well, daughter, you boil the pasta, add the sauce, then eat'—I realized she was asking to learn about a process that she had casually observed countless times before."

As we participate in activities that are part of our daily routine, behaviors become so ingrained that we become less aware of the individual tasks, subtleties and events associated with the activity. Is there really any logical reason why many people throw spaghetti on the fridge to make sure it's fully cooked, when a simple taste would suffice? Behaviors or customs like this often go unnoticed—but from a designer's perspective, these behaviors are extremely important in gaining an understanding of how people actually live.

In this challenge created by Mark, reflect on how you take part in the common activity of cooking pasta.

> ## "Everything you see I owe to spaghetti."
>
> —Sophia Loren

 ## CHALLENGE

Using your powers of design, visually depict the various actions, sequences, tasks and behaviors in a one-page visual narrative that allows you to analyze and explain how you make pasta.

Consider all the steps, including tools, equipment and ingredients. Represent the activity from a variety of perspectives, showing the various stages, sequences and events. Focus directly on the process of the activity, thinking through all of the subtleties of behavior rather than the expected outcome.

TAKE IT FURTHER

Take the resulting visual narrative and use it to design something that would help create the ideal pasta-making experience—whether that's changing a step or two in your process, or actually creating a product that could aid you in your cooking.

1 Mark Baskinger created this layered visual narrative describing how he makes pasta with his daughter. For more examples of this kind of sketching activity, take a look at *Drawing Ideas,* which Mark co-authored with information designer and teacher William Bardel.

2 Jason May, one of Mark's students, incorporated all of the steps necessary for pasta making in a single sketch. Note the use of blue pencil to help establish the structure of each element; when photocopied in black and white, this draft preparatory work would disappear.

Check Me Out

 120 minutes 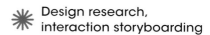 Design research, interaction storyboarding

If design is informed decision making, who decided to make the checkout at my local grocery store such a struggle? I think I'm going to switch to Aisle 6. Though the person at Aisle 3 only has ten items left on the conveyor belt. But it looks like they're having a good chat, which might delay things further. Or I could go through the self-checkout, but those machines always get upset at me. Besides, I need to buy a book of stamps.

Designers don't just make things. They also discover ways to improve systems. Waiting in line at the grocery store is one such system, which is contingent on a wide range of factors: the physical design of the store space, the placement and visibility of signage, the flow of people into and out of the checkout area and the computer systems that are used to scan items.

Take part in the following challenge, and see how you can systematically improve the grocery shopping experience for the world.

> "Supermarkets have evolved quite a bit from the corner grocery store, but they remain far from perfect. The constraints and compromises [made in placement of merchandise] are so contradictory and so complex that even a supermarket's supercomputer probably could not be used to solve the design problem in a way that would suit the storeowner and the shopper equally."
>
> —Henry Petroski, *Small Things Considered: Why There Is No Perfect Design*

CHALLENGE

Go to your local grocery store and observe the process of checkout from a number of different perspectives. Distill your notes into a user flow, sketching out the major considerations and events that happen through the checkout process.

Then, using that information, brainstorm comprehensive ideas regarding how you could improve the process of checking out—and how you could implement them at your local grocery store. What solutions, from ideal to feasibly real, would you propose?

TAKE IT FURTHER

Create a full-size, hand-sketched prototype of your auto-checkout solution, including any necessary interface elements. Then bring in test subjects to try out your prototype, and use their feedback to improve your design.

1,2 Claire Kohler spent an hour at the supermarket documenting the specific details that contributed to a person's checkout experience. From those notes, she created this poster that shows how a person would move through the process.

3

4

3,4 Mark Noterman and Claire Kohler considered what would happen if their local grocery stores had RFID (radio frequency identification) tags on all store items. By placing baskets on or pushing grocery carts underneath specially equipped tables, store visitors would have their purchases "rung up" and confirmed through a simple one-step payment confirmation process. This SmartBasket system would require effort on the part of food suppliers to provide the tags necessary to smooth out the checkout process, but it would definitely save time for customers when exiting the store.

The Game of Sustainability

⏱ 120 minutes ✳ Product design

Paper or plastic? Glass or aluminum? Eat local or buy foreign? When we are asked to make these kinds of decisions, the consequences of our actions are difficult to apprehend.

Take purchasing asparagus, for instance. You may be buying locally grown asparagus that was raised using hydroponics—which consumes power and water from your local utilities and watershed. Upon maturity, those vegetables were then driven one hundred miles to your farmer's market in a gasoline-powered truck and sold for a premium. Meanwhile, the delicious asparagus tips at your supermarket—flown to you from South America on a carbon-offset flight—were sun-grown, watered from a local river, certified organic by a third party, and processed in a wind-powered factory equipped with a fleet of biodiesel vehicles.

From these descriptions, any person would be hard-pressed to decide which asparagus was more or less sustainable. When it comes to issues of sustainability, there are few easy choices.

Now, imagine trying to describe the complexities of sustainability to a child. How could they even begin to comprehend the impact of their actions on the world? In the following challenge, you'll need to determine a way to help children understand the issue of sustainability.

TAKE IT FURTHER

How could you distribute your game to the world with the lowest impact possible?

"Sustainability is an approach to design and development that focuses on environmental, social and financial factors that are often never addressed. Sustainable solutions strive to improve the many systems that support our lives, including efficiently using capital and markets, effectively using natural resources, and reducing waste and toxins in the environment while not harming people in societies across the Earth."

—Nathan Shedroff, *Design Is the Problem: The Future of Design Must Be Sustainable*

❗ CHALLENGE

Create a simple game that teaches young children how to think about the natural resources they use as they go throughout their day. Consider the rules of play, whether the game would be a solo or group activity and what design choices you would need to make in order to best engage your audience. And one last constraint: The game has to demonstrate the principles of sustainability itself—by being eaten, recycled, composted or otherwise returned to the earth in the process of being played.

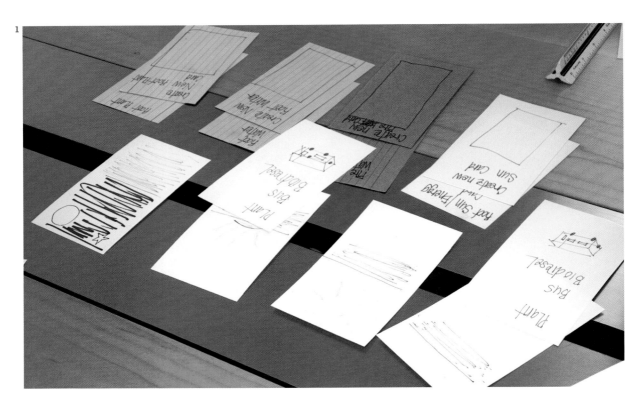

1 As part of an in-class brainstorm to solve this challenge, Shimon Alkon created a physical prototype of a card game. The different card colors represent resources, much like in *The Settlers of Catan*, and players follow what resources are used over the course of a day to manage the resources in their hand.

2 Over a lunchtime, my co-workers at frog design tried this challenge. One of the solutions, by Jake Zukowski, Abdullah Shaikh and Jeff Glasser, was a board game with waste pinned to particular spaces. If you land on those spaces, you have to pick up the waste and dispose of it.

3

3,4,5 Over two hours, I sat down and sketched out an idea for the game *WaterSource*, which would teach children about how to be mindful of water consumption. The game would be provided in an envelope that contained instructions, playing cards and printed wraps for drinking glasses from your home.

To play the game, you hold a hand of five cards—most of which represent daily activities that require water, such as cooking, playing in the park, showering and cleaning up. You then go around the table and play a card from your hand, pouring any water lost during your turn into a communal glass at the center of the table.

When that communal glass is full, the game is over and the player with the most water in his cup is declared the winner.

4

5

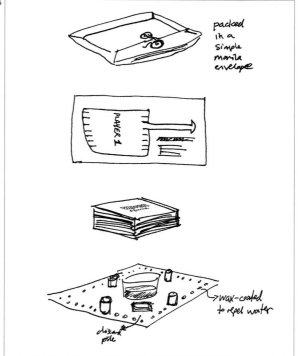

OBSERVATION

Take a look around you. You can't buy this at Hallmark.
Guided tour of your neighborhood, please. To vend or not
to vend. Just where is the emergency room? Imagine time
without your watch.

50 Patience, Grasshopper
51 Tour de Home
52 Wacky Vendo
53 Excuse Me, I'm Lost
54 Thinking Outside the Wrist

Patience, Grasshopper

 90 minutes  Illustration, research

Things in this world move too fast for words. Sometimes they just need to be observed. Sitting still, being present and noting people's behavior while withholding judgment: These underappreciated skills can have a powerful influence on our work. They bring forth the observations that give design a foundation in what we *know*, not just what we want or hope to uncover through the process of making.

With this challenge, you will be observing a problem rather than working to solve it.

CHALLENGE

Go and sit in a public place for one hour. Watch what happens. Empathize with what others around you are thinking, feeling and doing. When your hour is up, take the most potent thing you observed during that time period and express it in one of the few places reserved for pithy and poetic sentiment: a greeting card.

You cannot bring a notebook, camera, cell phone or any other type of digital or analog device to record your experience. Try not to think about what you're going to create until your time is finished.

> *"It is likely that sympathetic and empathetic skills are the most valuable in my toolbox. The ability to accurately see through the eyes of others, according to a defined context, allows a designer to craft a more appropriate presentation and experience. That experience is the whole reason design is necessary."*
>
> —Andy Rutledge

TAKE IT FURTHER

Write down the key experiences that formed the core of your greeting card concept. Is there a series of note cards, pads or other goods that could be created out of what you experienced? Or could you take your ideas further, into some form of digital expression in the interactive realm?

1 Claire Kohler took up residence on a bench at Green Lake Park in Seattle and observed what happened around her. Hearing conversation from walkers passing by, she imagined what the geese would be saying if they were talking as well. The interior reads, "Go ahead and leave the stroller and the dog at home, 'cuz hey, it's your birthday!"

high chair drum solo

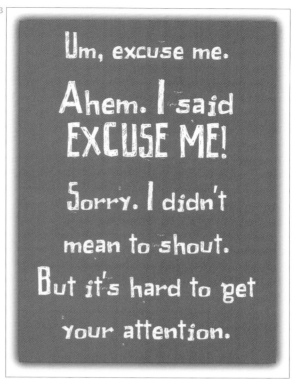

Um, excuse me. Ahem. I said EXCUSE ME! Sorry. I didn't mean to shout. But it's hard to get your attention.

2 Meg Doyle was spending time with her infant nephew when the idea for this greeting card hit her, along with perhaps some flying food. The inside says, "Happy Mother's Day. I hope you have peas and quiet."

3 Michelle Cormack sat on the steps of the Vancouver Art Gallery in Vancouver, British Columbia, for an hour on a Friday at lunch. "People were just busy walking on by, and nobody ever seemed to take a moment to just take it all in." Hence, the closing text in the interior of her card: "Put this card down. Go sit on your back step. Turn your face to the sun. And just stop."

4 Designer and illustrator Lisa Stewart sat in three different locations for inspiration. "The one that called to me were the fireflies. This is going to become a series of reminiscent images from childhood, but not necessarily nostalgic… While most greeting cards on the market speak of imminent milestones, this greeting card is not your typical greeting… I haven't seen many greeting cards that say, 'Enjoy Your Summer,' but it happens to be my favorite season of all."

Tour de Home

 120 minutes   Environmental signage, research

Within a mile of my house, there are a number of high-profile landmarks that I can't help but share with visitors to Seattle. The Fremont troll sculpture under the Aurora Bridge with a real Volkswagen Beetle clutched in one of his giant hands. The Woodland Park Zoo, with its crowd-pleasing penguins and flamingos. And let's not forget the organic and fair-trade chocolate factory.

All the places I just listed are what you'd call touristy—easily found in a Fodor's guide alongside every other big landmark in the Fremont district. As designers, we're often tasked with promoting these big-draw destinations.

But every local community, no matter how urban in nature, is full of unique and wonderful spots that have great meaning to its inhabitants—lovely locations that just wouldn't fit in the hundred-dollar guided bus tour.

For this challenge, you've been tasked with sharing these special places.

> **"Travel is the only context in which some people ever look around. If we spent half the energy looking at our own neighborhoods, we'd probably learn twice as much."**
>
> —Lucy R. Lippard, *On the Beaten Track: Tourism, Art, and Place*

CHALLENGE

Create simple, non-invasive signage that explains the provenance of the places you most often frequent in your community. What kind of information should you include to communicate the importance of each location to both locals and tourists? How can these signs be displayed in a manner that doesn't add visual noise to your entire neighborhood?

TAKE IT FURTHER

Design a piece of collateral for a neighborhood walking tour, complete with a simple map and callouts. Or, if you're looking for a big challenge, create a user interface for an iPhone app that can take you on a guided tour and point out the landmarks virtually— and allow you to create your own tour on the fly.

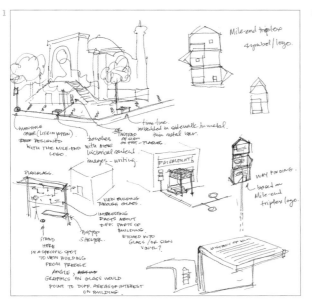

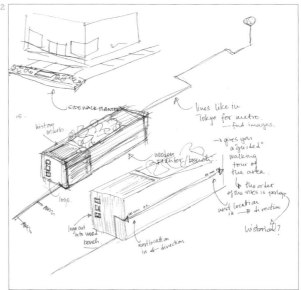

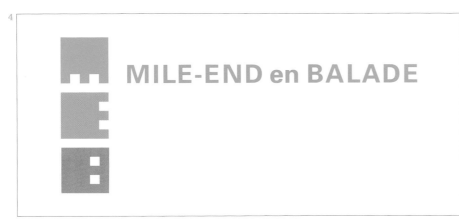

MILE-END en BALADE

1,2,3,4 For this challenge, designer Grace Cheong chose Mile End, a lively and diverse neighborhood of Montreal. "This area is known for its independent music and arts scene, cozy cafés and restaurants, cute little boutiques, its coffee and bagels and its architectural staple, the triplex… which is the base unit of the row housing that makes up most of the residential streets. The logo is inspired by the triplex form and by the bricks and stone that are the primary building materials in the area."

5,6 Grace devised her tour route: "An intertwining closed loop delineated by lines set into the sidewalk serves to direct the user on a casual walking tour of the area. One can join the 'tour' at any given point in the loop. Points of interest are marked by a custom wooden bench with planters. Each bench in the series is linked to the next by lines marked out in the cement leading you from one point of interest to the next. These benches serve not only as resting spots and sign posts, but also provide site history to the user and serve to add a little more green to the somewhat urban area. The engraved lines on the bench continue to join up with the lines marked out on the cement, leading you to the next location in either direction."

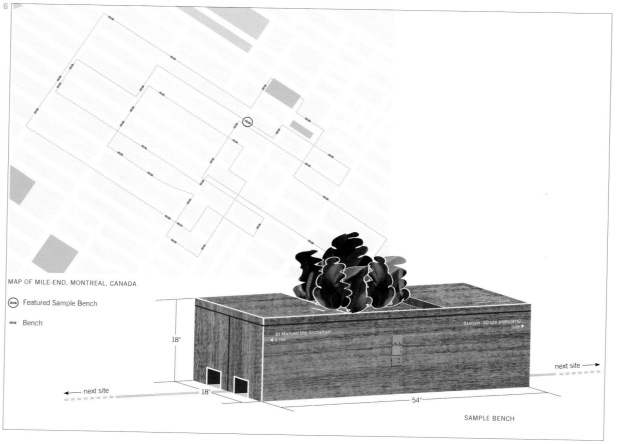

MAP OF MILE-END, MONTREAL, CANADA

Featured Sample Bench

Bench

18"

18"

54"

← next site

next site →

SAMPLE BENCH

Wacky Vendo

 120 minutes   Store design, product design

During a recent trip to Japan, I was stunned to discover the ubiquity of the vending machine. From Tokyo to Kyoto, there were *vendos* clamoring for attention on every train station platform and major street corner—almost one vending machine for every twenty-three people.

They don't use those machines to distribute solely snacks and drinks. From the necessary to the surreal, you never know what you'll find in those well-lit contraptions. Before you enter the Zen temple, would you like soda, juice, water, tea, coffee, beer or saké? Or, perhaps you would prefer underwear, ice cream, cigarettes, cosmetics, dirty magazines, MP3 players or tuna onigiri?

For this challenge, transcend the everyday vending machine by bringing the spirit of the *vendo* to your hometown.

> ## "Change is inevitable—except from a vending machine."
> —Robert C. Gallagher, retired chairman of Associated Banc-Corp

CHALLENGE

You've been asked by an industrial design firm to create a new kind of vending machine—one whose contents would fit the needs of your local neighborhood. What could you sell within this vending machine that would make sense for your local market, and how would you design the physical shape of the machine to stand out from the soda machines that we've all grown used to? Based on the contents of your machine, do you have unique space requirements? Will you need electricity in order to keep things refrigerated or heated? And how would you handle monetary transactions?

TAKE IT FURTHER

Take photos of spaces in your town where you'd include the vending machine, then retouch the photographs to include renderings of the machine. Are there any design modifications that you need to make when you see your vending machine in context?

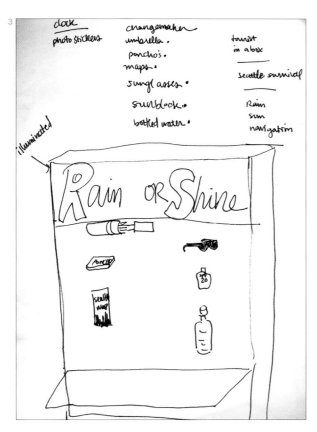

3

dock
photo stickers

changemaker
umbrella.
poncho's.
maps.
sunglasses .
sunblock.
bottled water .

tourist
in a box

seattle survival

Rain
sun
navigation

illuminated

Rain or Shine

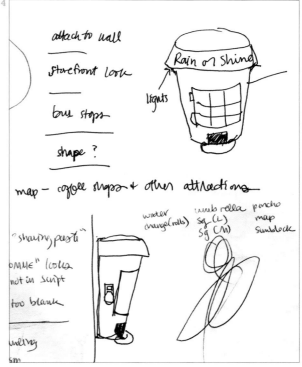

4

attach to wall

storefront look

bus stops

shape ?

map - coffee shops + other attractions

attach to wall
storefront look

Rain or Shine

lights

"shaving paste"

OMME" looks
not in script
too blank

water
change(rolls)

umbrella poncho
Sg (L)   map
Sg (M)   sunblock

anding
sun

1,2,3,4 From a group brainstorm in class, Katharine Widdows incubated an idea for the Rain or Shine vending machine. In this rendering, which shows the bus stop a block from Westlake Center in rainy downtown Seattle, tourists and locals alike can purchase suntan lotion, a map of the city, sunglasses, a rain slicker, an umbrella and so forth. One thing the vending machine doesn't serve, though, is coffee—for that, you'll need to walk half a block in any direction.

Excuse Me, I'm Lost

 120 minutes Typography, wayfinding

Working on environmental signage is fun, but it can also be a deadly serious business. Your design decisions can have a critical impact on other people's health and livelihood, especially when you're working within the health care industry. After all, no hospital staffer wants a suffering patient to wander around the parking lot, crying out: "Can you help me find the emergency room?"

So, if you've ever had the itch to rethink the signage in an important public space, this challenge is right up your alley.

> *"The rules of navigation never navigated a ship; the rules of architecture never built a house."*
>
> —Thomas Reid

CHALLENGE

You've been tasked by your local hospital to improve their internal signage system. Head over to the hospital and spend thirty minutes auditing their existing system, observing and sketching people moving through problem areas. If you find that you need to take photographs, please be sure to ask permission from the hospital staff.

When you're done, create a before/after example of how you revised a critical piece of signage for the better. Consider the information design of the signage, the physical placement of each indicator in the space, and other major factors that can be improved.

TAKE IT FURTHER

Think outside the signage. Expand your project from one location to make a recommendation for extending an entire wayfinding system across the hospital. As part of your process, design a set of symbols that can be easily applied (along with type) for people who may not be able to read or understand the local language.

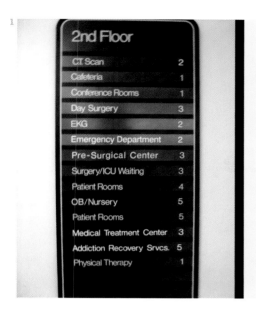

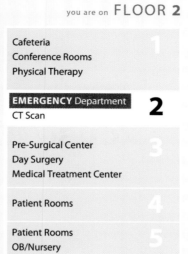

1,2,3 Katharine Widdows decided to rethink practically every aspect of the interior design and overall signage used in Swedish Medical Center in Ballard, a neighborhood of Seattle. By readdressing both the information design of the signage in the space and freshening the color scheme, she transformed a formerly dry and lifeless environment into a vibrant, lively space. It's also amazing that by typesetting the word "EMERGENCY" in white text knocked-out of a solid red background, she made locating the emergency room much easier.

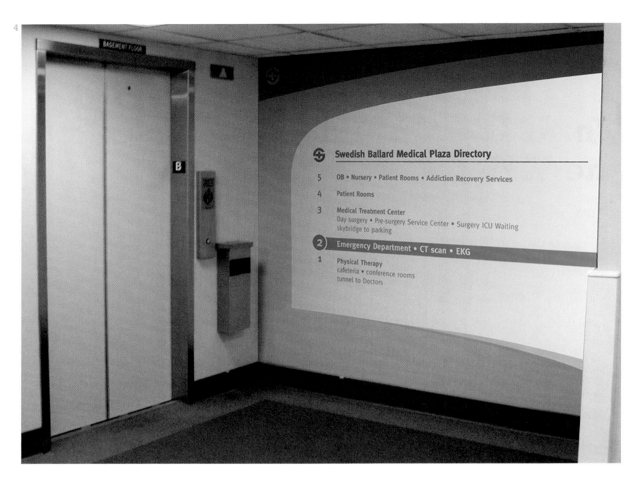

Swedish Ballard Medical Plaza Directory

5   OB • Nursery • Patient Rooms • Addiction Recovery Services

4   Patient Rooms

3   Medical Treatment Center
    Day surgery • Pre-surgery Service Center • Surgery ICU Waiting
    skybridge to parking

2   Emergency Department • CT scan • EKG

1   Physical Therapy
    cafeteria • conference rooms
    tunnel to Doctors

4 Mark Notermann looked at the same hospital photographs and imagined how much easier it would be for more people to read the directory simultaneously if the hospital directory took up the entire wall.

5 Jessica Thrasher added bold lines painted on the walls that a hospital visitor could follow to their intended destination. That way, hospital visitors would be oriented with regard to where they were going as they moved through the space.

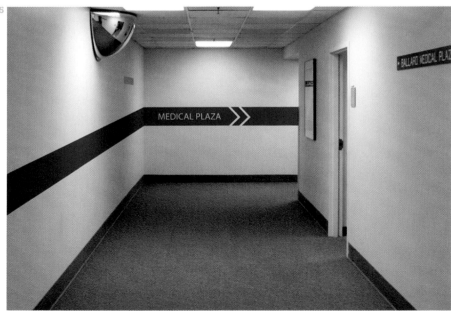

MEDICAL PLAZA

BALLARD MEDICAL PLAZA

Thinking Outside the Wrist

 120 minutes Research, product design, paper engineering

Time is a slippery fish for any creative professional.

From aggressive deadlines to daily schedules chock full of meetings, time is a rare commodity—and the unit of measure that governs our billings and profitability. Plus, designers yearn to submerge their minds for long stretches of design time, where they can ignore the ticking clock and luxuriate in the process of making.

In this challenge, however, you'll be asked to confront the role of time in your daily life—and to find ways that you can use your design thinking to bend it to your will.

> ## *"Day, n. A period of twenty-four hours, mostly misspent."*
> —Ambrose Bierce, *The Devil's Dictionary*

CHALLENGE

For one week, keep a diary about time. Every day, as you interact with your watch, phone, computer or clock, write down how you feel when you check the time. When the week is up, use the data that you gathered to design a "watch" prototype that redefines how people keep track of time—both in their day-to-day life, and in their pursuit of fashion.

What comes out of this exercise may not resemble anything like a watch at all. The watch may leave the wrist, merge with clothing, communicate via Bluetooth with phones or computers, etc. Because time is money, the cost of production on these watches must be fifty dollars or less.

Some good questions to ask before you begin designing may include: How did you feel about your watch/phone as you interacted with it? What would you change if you had unlimited control over time and space? How would you feel if your watch/phone was thrown out? And what would take its place?

TAKE IT FURTHER

Create a rudimentary physical prototype of your "watch" idea; carry it on you, and continue your diary study for a few days with the prototype. Does carrying the proto-type influence any of the details in your final design?

1

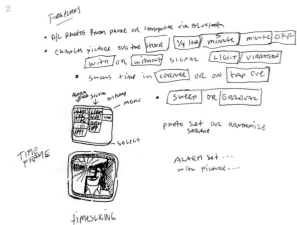

2

Features

- D/L photos from phone or computer via Bluetooth
- Changes picture on the [hour] [1/4 hr] [minute] [minute] [OFF]
  with [on] or [without] signal [LIGHT] [VIBRATION]
- Shows time in [corner] or on [trap cut]
  • [sweep] or [gradual]

photo set or randomize sequence

ALARM set ....
with picture....

TIME
FRAME

timeslicing

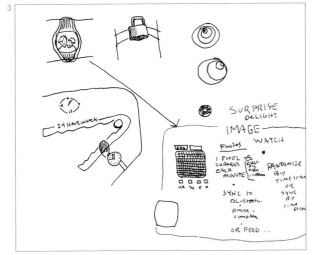

3

SURPRISE DELIGHT
IMAGE WATCH

photos

24 HOUR WATCH

1 PIXEL OR CHANGES EACH MINUTE   FULL OFTEN INTERVAL   RANDOMIZE BY TIME STAMP OR SYNC BY TIME STAMP

HR 4 5 0

SYNC TO BLUETOOTH
phone - computer

OR FEED ...

4

5

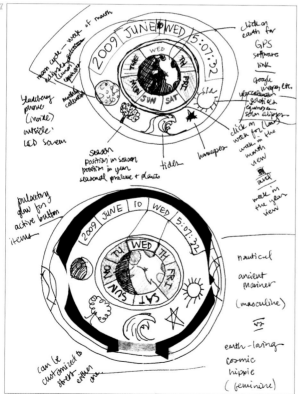

1,2,3 Mark Notermann's solution for this challenge was pictorial: "The SeeTime watch interacts via Bluetooth with a desktop app that allows you to build custom photo libraries or follow an online photo-sharing account. The watch would have a very simple touch screen that brings up the numeric time when you choose. In this view, the 'second hand' runs vertically in one-minute strips, which complete a full picture each hour. Options would allow for control of image flow and refresh rates, as well as visual alarms, reminders, etc."

4,5 Graphic designer and art director Tom Takigayama observed, "Due to technology (mainly mobile phones) where time is a built-in feature, the watch is no longer a necessity and has fallen back onto its other characteristic as a fashionable accessory. Convenience is the major draw for carrying around an all-in-one device. Aesthetics and its luxury value as a status symbol have saved the watch from becoming obsolete. The solution is the watch must become more convenient to compete with technology. The watch must stay branded as an aesthetic status symbol." From this design direction, Tom was inspired by the iPod shuffle and the classic form of the tie clip to create this sleek and stylish "modern watch" driven by LED lights below a mirrored face.

6,7 Katharine Widdows wanted to create a modern, touch-screen enabled version of the fob watch. Within that circular interface, users could visualize their location on a spinning Earth, see the phases of the moon, bring up tide tables, leaf through an almanac and explore other content that fosters one's connection with the planet.

INNOVATION

Making things better, as well as better things. Help define the "digital album." The iPhone frontier. Return your patio to Mother Nature. Buy less, consume less. Cooking with wine you really want to try. Can you contain your olive oil craving? Help your yoga mat talk with your Mac. This store doesn't sell anything. Text your coffee maker. Design your favorite dish. Bank on changing the world.

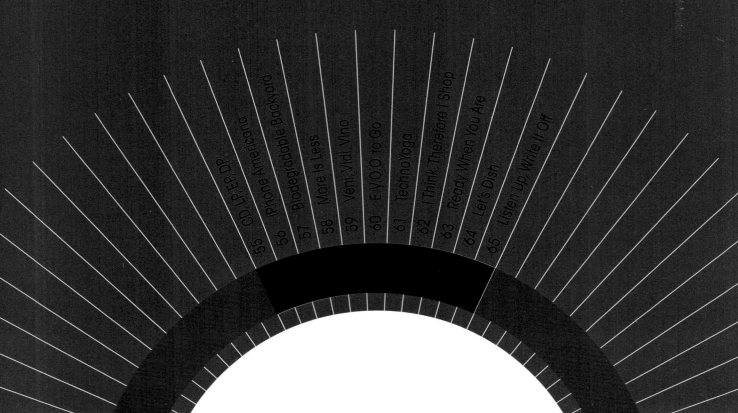

CD, LP, EP, DP

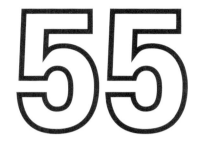

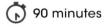 90 minutes    Interactive media

Imagine me in the seventh grade: a denim-jacketed youth trudging his way toward work at a candy store, Walkman blasting Guns N' Roses's *Appetite for Destruction*. Next door to my short-term employer was the Record & Tape Exchange, where I truly fell in love with graphic design.

From Hipgnosis's work for Pink Floyd to Vaughan Oliver's sleeves for the Pixies all the way to New Order's orderly layouts by Peter Saville, I feasted my eyes on lavish album packaging that spoke volumes regarding the music inside. I then spent the proceeds of my day job amassing a stockpile of my favorite album sleeves. (Oh, and the actual LPs were pretty good, too.)

While digital recording mediums and application platforms like iTunes have single-handedly destroyed the idea of music needing to be sold in a physical package, either as an LP or CD, there's still something to be said for the role of design in buying music. Visual and tactile stimuli will always contribute an additional dimension of meaning to songs.

In the following challenge, you will be asked to re-imagine the role of record packaging in the digital age.

CHALLENGE

Create a "digital package"—or DP—for a recording artist whose work you admire, but can't currently bring yourself to purchase online for $20.99. What kinds of content would you expect to receive at that price point? And how would that content be shaped by design to create a compelling music-listening experience?

> *"If the milk industry can make their product seem sexy and increase consumer demand, there must be hope for music."*
>
> —Gary Arnold, merchandising manager, Best Buy

TAKE IT FURTHER

Will your new invention single-handedly save the record industry? After you've designed a rough prototype of your idea, put together a business plan with infographics describing the impact of the DP on the recording industry as a whole.

1 Dave Fletcher, creative director at theMechanism, had the following simple solution to this challenge: "The concept of USB drives for the music industry isn't a new idea. However, by the small number of bands using the medium, and the number of labels who are not embracing it—it remains a fringe idea. Radiohead and the White Stripes have designed unique pieces of art in their USB drives, but I have attempted to demonstrate something that can be mass produced for a number of artists at once, either through bands forming a collective or via a label… I've tried to present a practical solution that artists can use now to increase the viability as well as the longevity of both the final designed product and the music itself. Unlike CDs that can be simply thrown out, these USB TRAC-PAC drives are reusable if wiped and also could be used to protect data from being shared."

2 With each USB TRAC-PAC purchase, you get the following:

- Full track list in MP3 format without DRM
- An unique image for each MP3 track
- .AIF uncompressed files for remixing
- Photographs
- Video files (accessible only through USB)
- Posters
- Link to online content that requires the USB key to be in the drive

Every new purchase should also provide a "free pass" to download the next album "as it's being recorded"—allowing fans to hear what goes into making an album.

The device would lock content, ensuring that the buyer needs to put the USB device into a computer to access certain content. Possible self-expanding files on the flash drive allow the user to copy only specifically determined files to the desktop, while additional movies and music extras must be played via the contained interface.

1

2

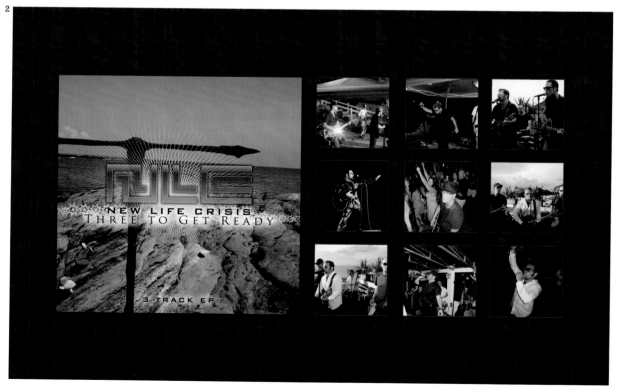

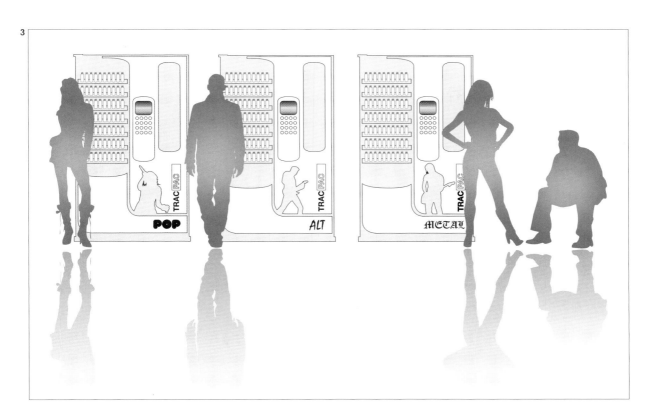

3 Vending machines could be anywhere, bringing a music store to the sidewalk, airport or concert venue. Unique, limited-edition live footage of the band performing could be placed into the machine at venues, adding to the concert experience. Customers could refill their USB TRAC-PAC as well, instead of always buying new ones.

4 Retailers who decide to not place USB TRAC-PAC vending machines in their stores could opt for simple and small packaging similar to phone cards. Packaging would be made from partially recycled paper to reduce waste.

iPhone Americana

 120 minutes 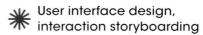 User interface design, interaction storyboarding

Every time a new device platform enters the smart phone market, there's a land rush for the creation of well-designed applications. Just look at the iPhone. The first speculators in the iTunes App Store introduced very simple games and applications and ended up reaping hundreds of thousands of dollars in downloads—mostly because there weren't many applications to choose from.

Times have changed, however. App designers fight for money and attention, even with the advent of the iPad. They attempt to coax ninety-nine-cent downloads out of increasingly skeptical customers whose devices are laden with low-utility applications that take up precious pixels of screen real estate.

In such an overloaded market, how could you cut through the clutter with a simple, compelling idea that's both useful and lucrative? In this challenge, you'll explore the wild new frontiers of mobile application design, but with a nostalgic twist.

TAKE IT FURTHER

Does it make sense to extend your idea into a piece of desktop software, a web application, or onto the iPad? See if there are opportunities to take your ideas beyond the iPhone.

 CHALLENGE

Devise a user flow and user interface for an iPhone application designed to take the place of a real-world physical activity that's rooted squarely in Americana. As an example: You could craft a jukebox application that plays blues and country music culled from your iTunes library—complete with bubble tubes and rotating colored lights.

As you're working through the details of your application, be sure to consider its feasibility, potential market, and the price point it would need to be sold at to turn a profit with a few thousand purchases.

"The Internet is like a gold rush; the only people making money are those who sell the pans."

—Will Hobbs

1,2,3 When traveling to exotic, quirky or surreal locations, it's common to send postcards off to your friends and loved ones that capture your experience. But instead of trolling the touristy gift shops around Mount Rushmore or Wall Drug for two-dollar postcards, you can snap a photo with this iPhone application by frog design and *voilà*, send a custom digital postcard to as many people as you desire.

 **Biodegradable Backyard**

 120 minutes   Product design, research

Lying in the backyard, reading a book and relaxing in the sun one day, I was suddenly struck by how practically every product within eyesight was designed to outlast me.

Green plastic deck chairs, rippled to simulate wood grain. A plastic bird feeder—a popular speakeasy for the starlings and robins. In the garden, a pair of purple Crocs shoes were lurking near the tomato plants, whose vines wound happily around black plastic stakes. Even the snakelike garden hose tucked between the bushes has been explicitly designed to resist the elements, no matter the long-term environmental cost.

For this challenge, rethink the logic that governs how we produce products for outside our home.

> *"Until man duplicates a blade of grass, nature can laugh at his so-called scientific knowledge."*
> —Thomas Edison

 CHALLENGE

Pick an item that you'd generally find in your backyard—such as one of the items in the above list—and redesign it so it could gracefully biodegrade. As an example, consider the bird feeder. Could you make such a thing that also wouldn't be torn asunder by hungry birds over a single season, or ravaged by the elements? Or is that part of the conceit, that you want the feeder to eventually be eaten?

TAKE IT FURTHER

Think about how you would brand and market your new product to encourage people to choose biodegradable products for their backyard. Or, if you're feeling adventurous, construct a physical mockup of your idea, place it within your garden and document over time how it returns to nature.

1,2 In tackling this challenge, designer Brian LaRossa came up with BirdBloom, a birdhouse that is water-resistant on the outside, but when inverted and left out in the garden, naturally biodegrades and returns to the earth. The bright colors would be sure to attract our fine feathered friends.

3 One of the inspirations for this challenge was "Bird Seeder" by industrial designer Jan Habraken. She says her birdhouse, which is made entirely of bird seed, is an example of "super functionality." In her design, she "strip[s] away everything unnecessary to function—and leaves something lyrical. Function becomes foundation becomes façade."

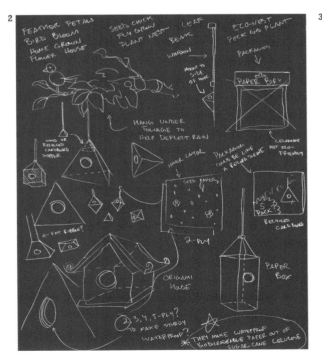

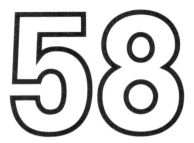 **More Is Less**

 90 minutes   Packaging, paper engineering, physical prototyping

Living within your means can often be hard, especially in a society that courts consumerism. Concepts like portion control, green living and thinking local for our weekly produce needs seem entirely feasible in our minds.

Then we find ourselves wilting when confronted with a Costco-sized bargain. *Of course I need twenty rolls of paper towels.*

Whether we like it or not, we contribute to this dialogue between the consumer and the consumed. Far too often, we abdicate our societal responsibility in the name of design. And as consumers ourselves, we find it hard to resist splurging on what might be—for our world's future—a wasteful purchase.

For this challenge, help to reduce that waste!

"Globally we are approaching the point when the only sustainable way forward is to want less. Indeed, the choice element may be removed from us and we will just have to have less."

—Don Johnston, chair, Solent Energy & Environment Group

CHALLENGE

Choose a product that you regularly use as part of your day-to-day life—food, drink, cleaning supplies, paper products, etc.—and determine a way to redesign or repackage it so consumers will want to use less of it.

How can you use your design skills to make more out of less, and encourage people to use that reduced quantity in a more mindful manner?

TAKE IT FURTHER

Create a physical mockup of your packaging idea, and see if your new packaging format helps you and others use less of the product.

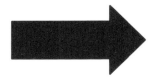

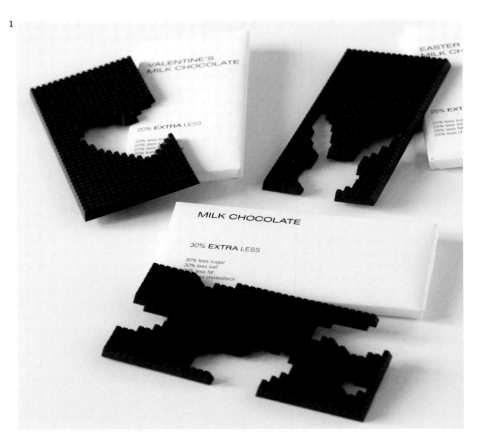

1

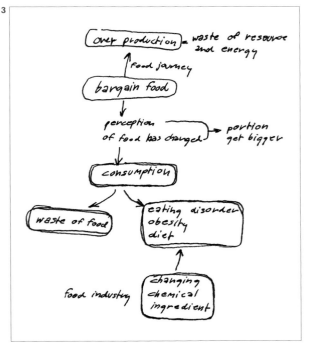

2

3

1,2,3 The inspiration for this challenge came from industrial designer Tithi Kutchamuch, whose project "My Sweets" reimagines our relationship to bargain food. "I buy Twix Extra because it's only ten pence more expensive than the regular one. I finish it in one go, and feel guilty for the rest of the day… Bargain food persuades people by playing with the value of money, which has brought a lot of problems to society: over-nutrition, eating disorders, obesity, illness, guilt, wasting food, wasting resources, over-production, etc. Can design make people buy food that offers *less*?" In this project, Tithi proves that this is possible in an aesthetically pleasing way.

4
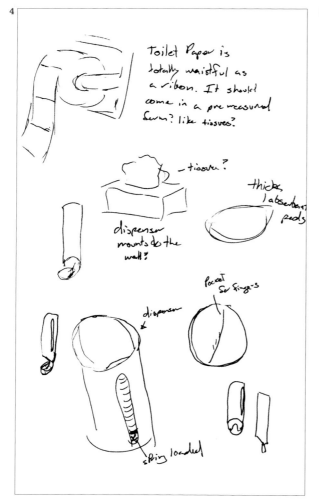

Toilet Paper is
totally waistful as
a ribon. It should
come in a pre-measured
form? like tissues?

— tissue?

thicker
absorbent
pads

dispenser
mounts to the
wall?

Pocket
for fingers

dispenser

spring loaded

5

4,5 Designer Katie Greff considered
ways for people to use less paper
when in the bathroom. By rethinking
how toilet paper is dispensed—in
individual two-ply circle-shaped
wipes that have a half-fold on the
back—people will be encouraged
to use it more sparingly.

Veni, Vidi, Vino

 30 minutes  Packaging

When I shop at the corner store for a wine to go with dinner, I'm always drawn to a grand display of artful bottles. Witty wordplay, embossed and die-cut labels, colored glass and paper substrates, hand illustration and calligraphy—the ways a designer can customize wine packaging are endless.

So, what about when I'm selecting a cheap wine that I plan on using in the meal as part of the recipe? That's a little easier, though I may not be satisfied if I try to *drink* it. Why isn't there an affordable wine that's great to sip, but is cheap enough that you feel fine about pouring a glass into the stir-fry?

In the following challenge, create the packaging for this elusive wine buy.

> *"I cook with wine, sometimes I even add it to the food."*
> —W.C. Fields

CHALLENGE

Create the packaging for a red table wine that balances taste, affordability and visual wit. Come up with the name of the winery, sketch out a label idea and choose the bottle substrate. Ideally, your bottle design should be simple enough that it can be versioned based on different varietals (Cabernet Sauvignon, Merlot, Malbec, etc.). No matter how good the wine tastes, the label has to be tasty enough to our eyes for a purchase to make sense.

TAKE IT FURTHER

Your new wine is so cheap—and high quality!—that your distributor wants to provide it to consumers in bulk. How can you package your design so the bottles can be distributed and sold in units of six? Or do you need to rethink your initial packaging concept as a box or 1.5L magnum?

1

2

3

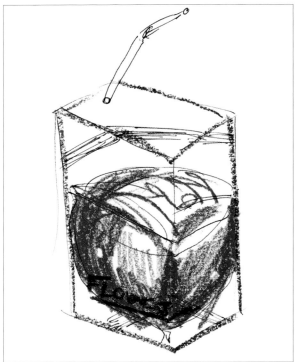

4

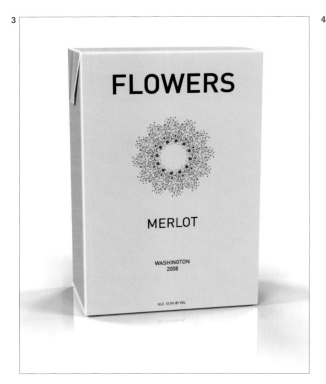

164

1,2 In a twenty-minute class brainstorm, Michelle Cormack and I quickly hit upon the idea of placing two different kinds of wine in one container: 250ml for cooking and 500ml for drinking. This presented some mechanical challenges for us, as we wanted a paper container for easy recyclability. And it was also interesting to see if we could include white wine and red wine in one container—this was a risk, as the customer would have to be comfortable with the red wine being chilled. We thought of way to sidestep this, however, by explicitly asking the customer to use the lower-grade wine for meals such as *coq au vin* and *beef bourguignon*, the recipes for which were printed directly on the package. Once that design strategy was put into place, the logo and design of the package came together quickly.

3,4 Donnie Dinch and Mark Notermann conceived of Flowers Wine, whose simple modern style hints at the fresh, fragrant nature of the affordable wine within.

5 *Vingt-et-un* means twenty-one in French—and it's also the name of a popular game of chance. But designer Aynex Mercado chose this motif because "my birthday is on March 21, and we believe in my family that the number 21 is important... I decided to go with this design because I thought it was the most eye-catching on the bottle, even though [my initial explorations that] used 21 as the shape of the label were more interesting."

6 Having a little fun during a twenty-minute collaborative brainstorm with Meg Doyle, she and I sketched out a series of wine bottle labels that showed the mishaps that ensue when having drunk a little too much wine. Hence, Wine-Oh! It's unlikely that they'll let us stock this brand at the convenience store.

 **E.V.O.O. to Go**

 30 minutes Product design, reasearch, packaging

What do the words "simple luxury" mean to you? Is it a hop in the Bentley for a journey down Rodeo Drive, seeking a new $20,000 handbag? Or does it mean that at dinner you like to dredge your focaccia in olive oil mixed with balsamic vinaigrette and fresh-cracked black pepper?

The concept of luxury has changed dramatically over the past decade. People are seeking out smaller, more meaningful ways of pampering themselves—and they're willing to spend more on incremental purchases and everyday luxuries, rather than big-ticket items.

Which brings us back to olive oil. You can spend a few bucks for a bottle of common olive oil at your local supermarket, or throw down a few larger bills for a tiny vial of the cold-pressed high-grade oil made by Italian nuns who stomp the fruit with their feet.

Both a commodity product and a simple luxury, the act of buying quality olive oil is becoming much like the high-end salt market. Did you know there are foodies who carry around little wood boxes containing special high-grade salts to enhance the flavor of their meals? They may be on to something.

For the following challenge, you'll help people carry around their high-grade olive oil, too.

> *"Olive oil? Asparagus? If your mother wasn't so fancy, we could shop at the gas station like normal people."*
>
> —Homer Simpson

! CHALLENGE

A local Italian restaurant wants to roll out a product that allows gourmet eaters to sprinkle their exceptional olive oil onto their favorite dishes while they're at home or on the go—and they need a product designer to help them figure out how to make it happen.

While this may seem like a simple problem on the surface, there are many issues that need to be considered. Since olive oil is perishable, how much oil can be stored and used before spoilage occurs? What will keep oil from oozing out of the package and soiling what's around it? What would make this product refillable? What materials would you select to make it sustainable?

And, most importantly—what attributes of your design will make the product feel like a desirable luxury item?

TAKE IT FURTHER

Design a print advertisement for a luxury magazine that shows your proposed bottle design in action.

Exercise 60

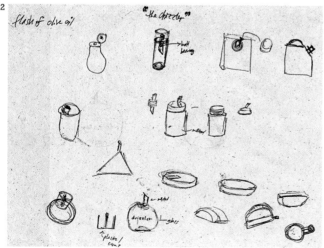

1,2 Over twenty minutes in class, Donnie Dinch and I brainstormed the idea for the Drizzler, an easy-to-grasp olive-shaped container with a pop-out spout that would make it easy to pour olive oil without it getting all over the product.

3 In contrast to the sleek sophistication of the Drizzler, Mark Notermann and Meg Doyle came up with a simple idea: Repurpose Visine-style bottles designed to squeeze out a few drops of a liquid substance, silkscreen them with the appropriate product information, then for an added bonus toss in Mr. E.V.O.O.'s good friend B.V.

TechnoYoga

🕐 120 minutes ✳ User interface design, information architecture

My daily yoga routine begins with the *Dandasana*, or Staff Pose—in case you don't understand Sanskrit. This is followed by a series of Sun Salutations, ending in Downward-Facing Dog with a transition into a series of standing poses (Warrior 1, Side-Angle Pose and Triangle Pose). And the sequence always ends with a meditation in Corpse Pose, or *Shava-asana*.

No matter whether you're a frequent practitioner of yoga or a beginner, there is a specialized language—both spoken and physical—that must be learned to develop a yoga practice. Most of us start through in-person instruction as part of a large group. Our teacher guides us through the details of specific poses. Over time, we learn how to string those individual poses together into a sequence. We can then take our practice anywhere and conduct it on our own.

I enjoy practicing yoga at home, but there are great benefits that come from interacting with a teacher and class. Is there a way that I could practice yoga at home with the help of a (digital) personal instructor? Find out in the following challenge.

> *"A photographer gets people to pose for him. A yoga instructor gets people to pose for themselves."*
>
> —Terri Guillemets

CHALLENGE

Create the user interface for a web application that wirelessly communicates with your yoga mat and tracks what poses you've attempted over the course of your daily practice.

This application could also suggest to you what poses you'll like best for variety based on what discipline of yoga you enjoy (Hatha, Vinyasa, Iyengar, etc.), or a blend of different disciplines, or even what people similar to your body type or lifestyle have also enjoyed.

TAKE IT FURTHER

Design the mat that would go along with the web application. What material and technologies would be required to create seamless communication with your computer?

1,2,3,4 I first articulated the following principles to help frame the execution and steer my sketching.

You will be guided when using this yoga application, but you also need to be in your body and focused.

You want the input of others, but don't want to be forced into having their physical presence in the room.

The application would need to see how you settle into the practice and would adjust over time.

I began sketching and had the idea to portray each yoga session as a mandala pattern. The person using the app and the specially wired yoga mat would be able to track her movement from pose to pose by breath (not time), and she could easily pause, move to the next pose or shift back into child's pose. The app would then adjust the routine based on actions, changing the number of breaths per pose necessary to complete the entire session.

Small infrared sensors in the corners of the mat would track the user's body movements when her hands or feet were not on the mat, and after the yoga session, the user could see whether there were any poses that exhibited mechanical issues that could lead to injury.

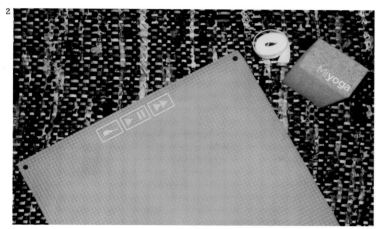

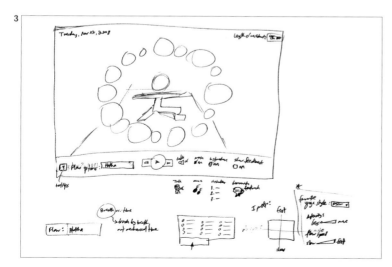

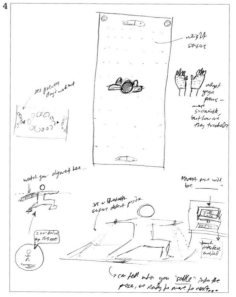

 I Think,
Therefore I Shop

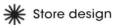 90 minutes Store design

Wandering through an open-air mall on a blustery spring day, you can't help but notice the window shoppers lingering outside a chef's store.

In the window displays, silicone cake pans stacked in a bold pattern jockey for space alongside a stainless-steel mixer that looks like an *objet d'art*. Observing the ways the shoppers around you graze the information contained in the display, you can see how effective display design isn't solely about the product. First, you need to sell an idea of what lifestyle could be attained *with* that product.

But what would happen if you were only selling the idea itself—not tangible, physical things?

CHALLENGE

You've been asked to plan and create a retail store that sells ideas instead of physical, take-away objects. In your explorations, consider its naming, overall branding and signage.

Exactly what kinds of ideas would exist there, and how would they be made manifest for "purchase"? How would you approach constructing such an experience? What role would design take in making it? Finally, how would you want visitors to change their behavior after visiting such a place?

"If the financial crisis was caused by the over-consumption of things we couldn't afford and the environmental crisis is being caused by the over-consumption of things we can't afford and the health crisis is being caused by the over-consumption of things we can't afford, then it points toward there being a bit of a problem with endless consumption. So what's the alternative?"

—Tim Brown

TAKE IT FURTHER

Create a physical prototype of the experience, including an elevation of the store experience and examples of what artifacts would be necessary within the space to make people "consume" the ideas in an expedient fashion.

1,2,3,4,5 An inspiration for this challenge was the WANT store created by Donica Ida, Terry Liu, Francis Luu, Ivy Sa and the teacher Kristine Matthews in the University of Washington's environmental design class. WANT is a store experience designed to help college students develop smarter spending habits and become more savvy about their college finances. In WANT, goods are substituted with advice on how college students can save money. The "merchandise" inside the imaginary store is constructed from laser-cut cardboard, and includes everything from coffee to electronics to apparel, each printed with a different tip on how to save money on that item. As in a regular store, visitors are invited to flip through clothing racks and browse the shelves at their leisure. Visitors come away not with lighter wallets, but with better buying power.

6

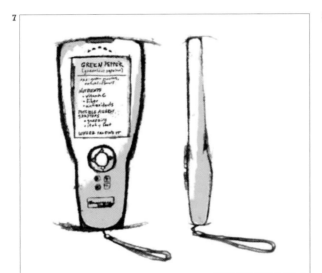

Knowcery
food detectives

7

8

9

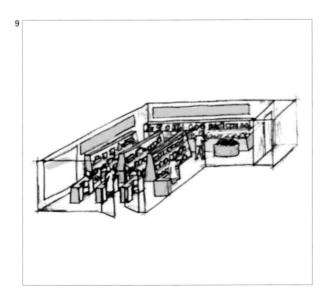

6,7,8,9 A team of students from one of my classes—including Shimon Alkon, Michelle Cormack, Jake Rae, Jessica Thrasher and Katharine Widdows—took on this challenge and created Knowcery Food Detectives, an integrated in-store and online experience that shows food allergy sufferers how to grocery shop with confidence. Modeled after a neighborhood grocery store, visitors can roam the aisles at their leisure and scan the barcodes of packaged and prepared foods, cleaning supplies, toiletries and pharmaceutical products to see full details regarding possible allergens.

Ready When You Are

 90 minutes 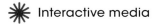 Interactive media

In this age of Internet-enabled gadgetry, I wouldn't be surprised if my refrigerator started talking to my toaster. Formerly dumb devices that crowded our kitchens and bedrooms are now driven by embedded operating systems instead of rudimentary circuit boards. This allows us a level of unimaginable integration between all of the things that surround us.

Which brings up a great question: What will we do with all this power? Most of us couldn't program our VCRs, let alone these newfangled digital video-recorders, and I just had a five-minute argument with my microwave regarding how to defrost vegetarian chili. (I lost.)

It's up to us—the designers of the world—to help shape the future of how humans interact with these fancy machines. And we should start with the most important appliance known to man: the espresso maker. With this challenge, put all this newfound connectivity and control to great use.

> **"In Seattle, you haven't had enough coffee until you can thread a sewing machine while it's running."**
>
> —Jeff Bezos

 **CHALLENGE**

You've been asked by Nespresso, the manufacturer of classy espresso makers that depend upon coffee capsules instead of loose grounds for their perfect output, to create a web application that lets people control their espresso maker via the Internet.

What kind of ways would you *want* to provide this kind of power to the everyday espresso drinker? What would this web application look like? How would it be deployed? Would it be just for you, or would you be able to participate in a virtual espresso-loving community? Pour yourself a cappuccino and get to work.

TAKE IT FURTHER

Determine how you would promote the rollout of this web application for the greater Nespresso community. Would you tease it on their web site? In their stores? And how would your overall grand vision translate into other cultures, languages and markets?

1

2

3

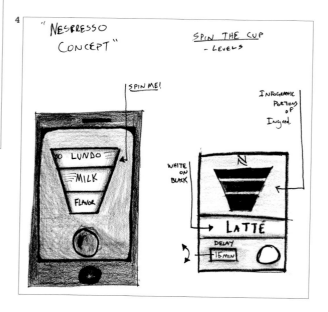

4

1,2 Mark Notermann created an iPhone application, the iBarista, which "extends the coffee connoisseur's experience beyond the last sip. The espresso capsule would leave a digital stamp when utilized in the brewing machine. This would be sent via Wi-Fi to the owner's online account where data would accumulate about the user's drinking habits. The user can rate his brews, and orders can also be automatically created with this data.

Another feature would enable meeting invites to be synched to their calendar, with the guest able to pick from a menu of espresso choices."

3,4 Donnie Dinch's solution exploits the touch interface of the iPhone to allow anyone with his app and the appropriately equipped espresso maker to pinch and choose the level of foam, milk and espresso desired in their latte, cappuccino or other coffee beverage.

Let's Dish

 120 minutes    Product design

The plain white bowl rests all alone on the kitchen table, awaiting your desired input. In the morning, you fill it with strawberry yogurt, nuts and granola. In the evening, your spoon clinks against the rim as you slurp down red lentil soup drizzled with mint-infused olive oil.

When designing products for our kitchen, such as plates, bowls and cups, we intentionally create shapes humble enough to fit any context. We are trained how to utilize them at an early age. And over time, we learn to adapt the use of those products to more narrowly defined needs. In this challenge, consider how you can do just that—and create something artful and extraordinary as a result.

> *"Products never speak for themselves. Someone had to teach us that a chair is meant for sitting on, that a spoon is for putting food into the mouth."*
>
> —Paul Mijksenaar and Piet Westendorp, *Open Here: The Art of Instructional Design*

CHALLENGE

You are a famous ceramics designer tasked with an unusual request: Come up with a way to reinvent a dish, cup, bowl or glass for one extraordinarily specific use. Don't aim for maximum utility. Instead, fulfill a need for dining ware you've always wanted in your cupboard, whether it's a plate designed to manage your portions at dinner or a cup with a lemon squeezer included for your lemon tea.

While you're at it, try to incorporate sustainable materials into your design, so your creation can return to the earth after it outlives its use.

TAKE IT FURTHER

After you've determined your ideal dish design, how could you brand, package and sell it in a sustainable manner? Does your initial idea suggest any further ways to extend your thinking into flatware?

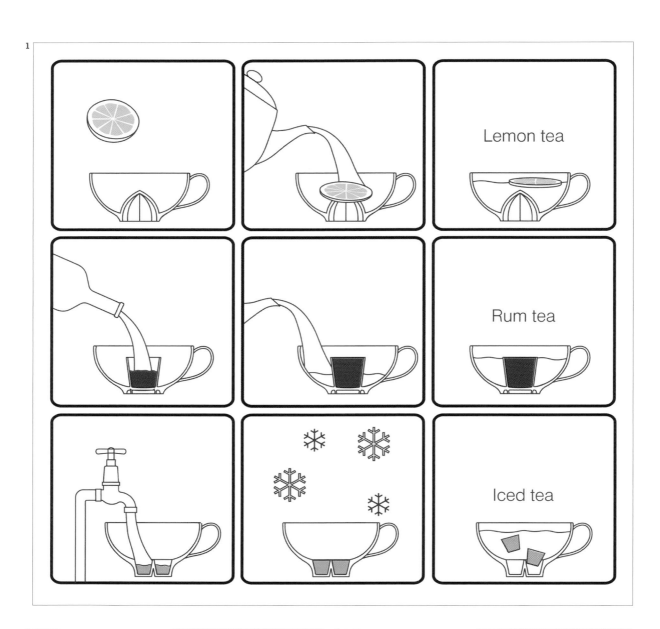

Exercise 64

4

1,2,3,4 Industrial designer Tithi Kutchamuch provided the structure for this challenge with her project "A cup of…" In this project, Tithi created teacups whose forms were contingent on specific types of tea: lemon tea, rum tea, iced tea and so on. "Each drink has its own typology of vessel, e.g., beer mug, wine glass, coffee cup, milk bottle, etc. [But] how about when we mix the drinks? [Mixing] two typologies creates a new function and ritual of drinking… [and] symbolism at the bottom of the cup."

 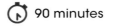

Listen Up, Write It Off

 90 minutes ✳ Out of home advertising

No matter how hard we try to tune out its siren song, advertising has a role in our society. The Ad Council, the largest national nonprofit producer of public service announcements (PSAs), is the undisputed king of wielding the copywriter's pen for public interest. Participating advertising agencies are tapped by the Ad Council to use their same techniques of persuasion employed in ads for everything from Snuggies to SUVs to asking us to stop forest fires and reduce the spread of H1N1.

Want to pitch in? Take part in this challenge and use your advertising savvy to create a worthwhile campaign that would fit in with the Ad Council's legacy.

> *"I always wondered why somebody doesn't do something about that. Then I realized I was somebody."*
>
> —Lily Tomlin

CHALLENGE

The team at your office came up with an idea for a "volunteer bank." This would be a web site where you can register your personal information and causes that you'd like to support. Then, nonprofit organizations can "check out" people who are interested in donating their time to those causes. In return for your time donation, you'd receive donated awards from the web site.

Now, you don't need to design the actual web site. What's more important is the question: How would you advertise it? Determine how you'd describe the volunteer bank—including name and identity—and then create a bus shelter advertisement that encourages people to go online and start donating time.

TAKE IT FURTHER

Write a thirty-second radio spot that describes the experience of checking out a volunteer.

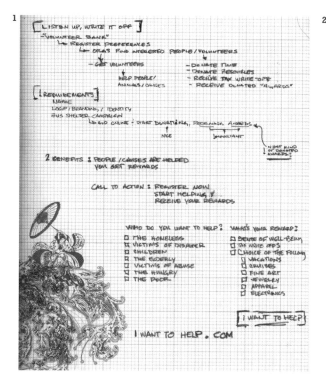

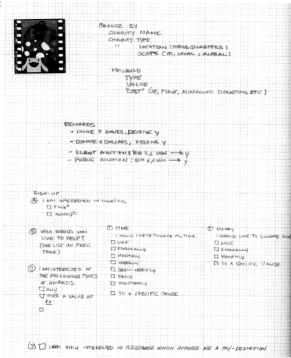

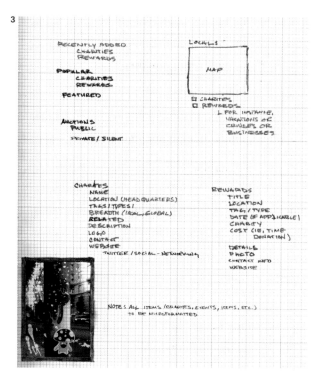

1,2,3 Tim Aidlin, a user experience designer at Microsoft, took on this challenge and designed his advertising concept around JustCauz.org. "Currently, JustCauz.org is a charitable organization based in Seattle geared toward social events with the proceeds going to two specific charities. It's our hope to move in the direction that this challenge describes in the near future, with JustCauz.org becoming a service and site dedicated to connecting volunteers with organizations who need help.

"The site would feature simple, straightforward methodologies to provide potential volunteers a way to specify their preferences on how they volunteer or help. For instance, volunteers might want to donate time or money. Volunteers might want to donate only one time, while others would like to be part of a group that meets every week. Volunteers might want to help with specific causes, such as children, the elderly, the homeless; or they might want to volunteer with particular organizations such as groups that are focused locally, rather than internationally."

4 Tim Aidlin continues, "The service provides charitable organizations a way to connect with interested potential volunteers who have expressed interest in criteria that fits your charitable organization.

"JustCauz could also work with all sorts of organizations to procure donated 'rewards' with which we then can award volunteers, based on some criteria, such as number of hours volunteered, amount of money gifted, number of members you've referred, etc.

"There is also the potential for auctions, both silent and public for items. Think eBay for charity."

4

180

INTERPRETATION

Think outside the… wait, where'd that box go? Reinvent the dollar store. Start a sock frenzy. Diapers gone wild! See what other people aren't. Gaze into that arty crystal ball. Make illustrations that look cheap. Is fancy Antarctic bottled water really such a good idea? Get in touch with your Buddhist blogger. Don't be blind to sunburn. Hearing-impaired people can rock out too. Welcome to the Museum of Smell. Turn up that television. That transit map took a weird turn. Just call it Twitterpedia. You wrote the book on it.

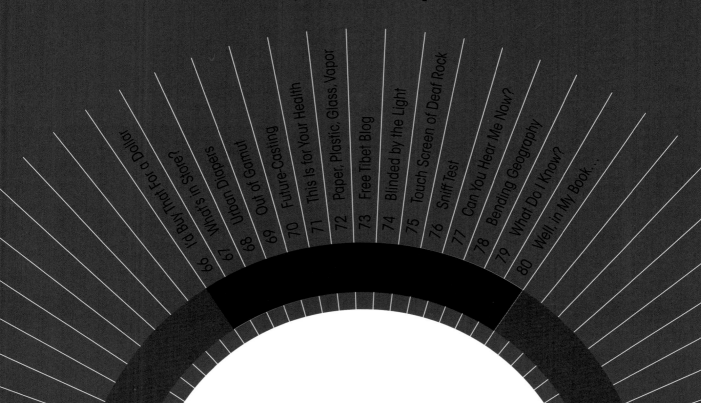

I'd Buy That For a Dollar

🕐 90 minutes ✳ Store design

Say the words "dollar store," and what comes to mind isn't high design. These booming businesses are the undertakers of retail, reselling what didn't shift from store shelves for pennies on the buck: packets of one hundred plastic straws, red and blue rubber balls dusted with glitter, half-gallons of milk and orange juice, and so forth. In a dollar store, you might find things you need, but your purchase is unlikely to be something you'd be proud to own.

Can you change that? Take on the following challenge and find out.

CHALLENGE

A startup incubator has tasked you with rethinking the very concept of a dollar store. Consider ways in which you can rebrand, restock, and otherwise reinvent a dollar store to provide products that are essential, sustainable and desirable.

After you've done your initial brainstorming, you should be able to describe the overall positioning of your store, provide a name and identity for the store, and visually describe what the store space would look like.

> *"America is the country where you can buy a life-time supply of aspirin for one dollar and use it up in two weeks."*
>
> —John Barrymore

TAKE IT FURTHER

If you choose to create physical products for your store, design a consistent packaging system for them, considering what kinds of substrates would be affordable and recyclable.

1,2,3,4,5 Designer Brent Williams conceived of Greenie's Attic, an eco-friendly dollar store "that provides an affordable alternative to the mass-produced, chemical-heavy household items that we use every day. In addition, [the store] stocks hundreds of useful materials for use in your own DIY projects… from chicken wire and precut wood, to seedlings and succulents. Our monthly mailer has all the resources you need to do them yourself. Leave a smaller footprint on the environment and your wallet."

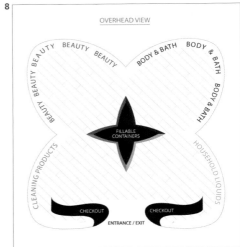

6,7,8 In a thirty-minute class brainstorm, a team that included Michelle Cormack, Jake Rae, Jessica Thrasher and Katharine Widdows came up with the idea of Nectar, a store that sells reusable, recyclable containers for a dollar that can be filled with a wide variety of cleaning, beauty, body and bath products—also available for a dollar per set amount of fluid ounces. The store interior would be arranged to resemble the shape and structure of a four-petaled flower, with plenty of space for customers to buzz about.

What's in Store?

 30 minutes  Retail store experiences

When you think of high-end retail store design, what companies come to mind? Perhaps Barneys New York, where you see dramatic displays that mingle high-end clothes with handmade sets that would look more at home in the Guggenheim Museum than a window overlooking Madison Avenue? Or is it the Apple Store, with its sleek modern lines and open spaces providing an architectural backdrop to the stunning industrial design of their products?

These companies specialize in creating visual poetry through artful arrangement. Foot traffic slows as shoppers stroll past. The doors beckon you to peek inside. It's almost like an invisible hook has snagged your elbow and hauled you face-to-face with a cashmere sweater that you don't need, but might want.

With the following challenge, prove that a well-crafted display can sell almost anything.

> ## *"A man is about thirty-eight before he stockpiles enough socks to be able to get one matching pair."*
> —Merrily Harpur

CHALLENGE

Can you create a store display that has the same stopping power as those examples noted above—but solely for high-end socks? As you work on your window display, decide on the name of the shop and the general look and feel of the entire storefront, including use of signage, awnings, logos or etchings on the windows, and any other important considerations that will contribute to the store's overall experience. And make sure your design will function cross-culturally. After all, markets such as Japan are sock-crazy.

TAKE IT FURTHER

Once you have the window display completed, devise a space plan for the store and how the store's contents could be arranged around your display.

LUXURY, FUN & CANINE SOCKS

1,2 Katharine Widdows and Michelle Cormack created a plan for Knit Wit, whose window display and hand-woven logo treatment is literally "off the wall."

3 In the allotted time frame, Mark Notermann and I brainstormed the name, logo, and overall design concept of Toe 2 Toe, a store that specializes in selling bright-hued socks woven from sustainable materials. The storefront would be floor-to-ceiling glass, and the centerpiece of the store would be a foot chandelier that illuminates a wide range of sock colors. The "sock boxes" shown stacked along the floor are made of 100% post-consumer waste and can be purchased to accompany gifts—and the proceeds could go toward charities that provide socks and shoes to those in need.

Exercise 67

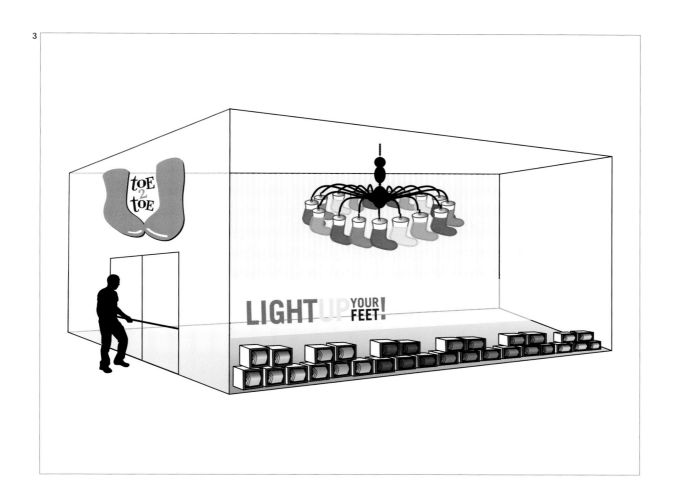

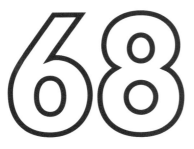

Urban Diapers

⏱ 60 minutes ✳ Identity development, packaging

If you're a parent, you know the joys of taking care of a child's needs until they've been potty trained. You are part of an elite brigade whose common bond is the ability to talk on the phone with one hand while taking care of a diaper with the other. As a designer, I've always wondered if there was a way to elevate the chic factor *and* the usability of what is otherwise a messy, multi-year responsibility. Can you be a new parent and look really good while taking care of number one and number two?

CHALLENGE

A client has approached you with an unusually creative brief (pun intended). You've been tasked with branding a line of baby diapers that caters to urban parents seeking an edgier feel to their baby care. Invent the name and logo for this new brand, then apply your identity to the diaper product itself, thinking through what type of packaging would be most appropriate for your target audience.

Can you take an accoutrement for an unappealing activity and make it more useful, sophisticated and cool?

> *"The reason we design things is to make them more effective and useful. It's about beauty, yes, but it's also about providing the client and customer the solution to their problem. Desire should emerge from the appropriate solution."*
>
> —David Conrad

TAKE IT FURTHER

Work out the finer details around the form factor, materials used, overall visual language, color palette, copy tone and description, and any other critical attributes of your new brand. Then marry all those details into a visual narrative to sell retailers on your visionary approach.

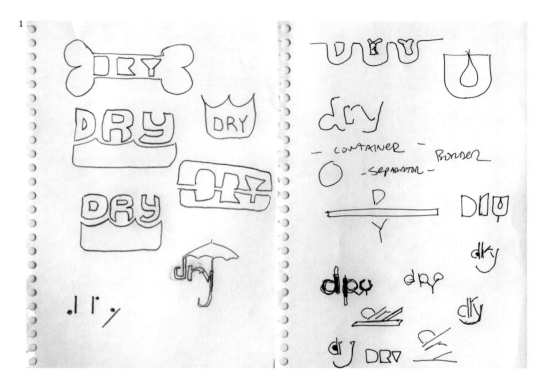

1,2,3,4,5,6 "Cry babies aren't dry babies." One of my classes, consisting of Donnie Dinch, Meg Doyle, Claire Kohler and Mark Notermann, took on this challenge and created a brand of diapers called Dry as part of a thirty-minute brainstorm. They envisioned the following messenger bag/diaper dispenser as a way to make diaper transport more hip. On the inside flap is a handy chart where you can keep track of when your baby does his or her thing. As part of their creative process, the team split apart and each person individually tackled a portion of the design: the identity design (1, 2, 3), the color palette and pattern (4, 5, next page), copy tone and brand voice, and the physical form factor of the bag (6, next page). Thanks to Jill Vartenigian for providing the initial idea that brought this challenge to life.

4

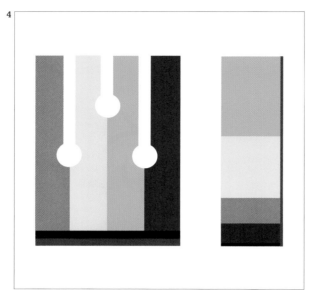

5

6

diaper
dispenser

Exercise 68

Out of Gamut

 90 minutes   Research, identity development

Do you see what I see?

As designers, we incorporate certain assumptions into our printed or online solutions. We work with the belief that certain words, images and colors will evoke predictable responses in the eyes of those who view them.

For the following challenge, this is definitely not the case.

> *"In visual perception a color is almost never seen as it really is—as it physically is. This fact makes color the most relative medium in art."*
>
> —Josef Albers

CHALLENGE

You've been hired by the National Association of the Color Blind to help them rethink their brand direction. Conduct the appropriate research, then present to your client for review the following deliverables: a new name for their nonprofit organization, a tagline that succinctly describes their new brand direction and a logo treatment that holds up in both solid and color-based executions.

Be prepared to speak to how their membership will view and interpret the brand materials. The most important thing your client wants to express in the new identity: "Helping people see the world through your eyes."

TAKE IT FURTHER

Put together a color study that explains how those with different types of color blindness will see your logo. Be sure to explore any potential variations between printed communications (reflected light) and online media (projected light).

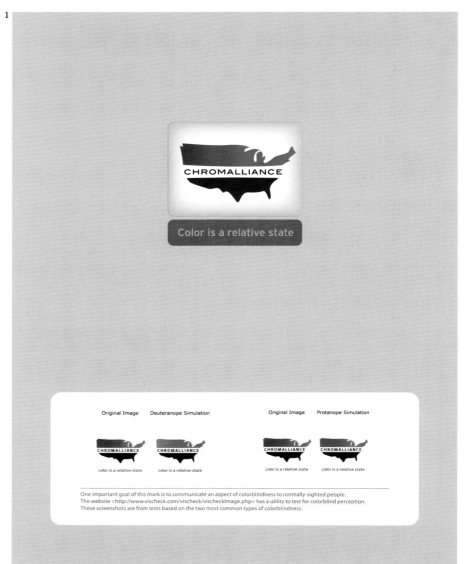

1 Mark Notermann's solution to this challenge was to create a logo and color study for the Chromalliance, whose tagline is "Color is a relative state." Mark said, "One important goal of this mark is to communicate an aspect of color blindness to normally sighted people." He recommended Vischeck (www.vischeck.com), which has a utility to test designs for color blind perception.

2 Full Spectrum: "Looking beyond the limits of vision." Jake Rae's take on this challenge was to have the logo assume the form of an Ishihara Color Test that was flying apart. His color scheme for the logo causes intentional friction with his name choice, as the red hues he used resemble those seen most differently by color-blind people.

Exercise 69

3

4

3 Michelle Cormack's design solution was for Spectrum—"Colour for all • all for colour." The letterhead and business papers provide a solid white space balance for a logo defined by a ribbon evoking the range of the visible color spectrum.

4 C-Lab: "Where seeing minds align." My approach to this challenge was to create a prism whose range of colors, in the overlaps and wobbly imbalance between primary hues, incorporated the more limited palette that would appear to someone who may be partially color blind. The black pupil in the center implies the shape of an eye.

70 Future-Casting

 60 minutes   Trade show

All too often, our clients are trapped in cold, hard business realities. Sell a million more widgets by Q4 and bring in twenty cents profit on the dollar. Conduct this rebrand so we can reap a 10 percent increase in our overall customer satisfaction rating. Keep up with the Ciscos and Coca-Colas of the world, and we'll be barely surviving.

Then there are clients whose aim is to not only participate as a day-to-day leader in their market, but also to anticipate their role in shaping the future. Part of the reason that these clients succeed is because they use the power of design to help determine their overall business strategy.

Never thought about what the future holds for your clients? Think creatively to form a possible long-term vision for a nonprofit institution in your area.

> ## "My interest is in the future, because I am going to spend the rest of my life there."
>
> —Charles F. Kettering, engineer and inventor

! CHALLENGE

You've been tapped by a modern art museum in your region to help them brainstorm a booth for next year's Art Basel Miami Beach, the most important art show in the world. The booth needs to sell to collectors, donors, artists and investors what the vision of the museum will be *five years in the future.*

Take thirty minutes to brainstorm big-picture concepts, then spring into action and execute your best idea as an architectural rendering, being aware of what materials and inputs are necessary to fabricate the experience.

TAKE IT FURTHER

Determine the logistics necessary, both in dollars and time, to ship, build and staff the booth for the four days of the show.

1,2 Designers Mark Notermann and Jill Vartenigian brainstormed the following ideas for a Seattle Art Museum exhibit in thirty minutes, which Mark then executed. "The concept for presenting a future for SAM is based on combining the element of random play as an act of creation, and digital media as a means of participation and connection. A kiosk with 'dirt boxes'—magnetically charged dirt-like material—would be the interface to control audio and visual output. Each participant would need to spend time in play, learning the interface, before becoming more deliberate with their audiovisual compositions. Two touchpad controls would allow them to wipe the display or save a static image to their e-mail address or phone as a keepsake."

3,4 In Jake Rae and Jessica Thrasher's take on this assignment, the future looks more like a dark alley filled with trash painstakingly recreated within the confines of a completely modern building.

This Is for Your Health

 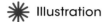 60 minutes ✳ Illustration

When looking at a gorgeous magazine illustration, have you ever had a feeling that it looked too good for the lack of an idea behind it?

Clever magazine illustrations, conducted with a high level of polish, can require elaborate, multi-day executions. But without a strong concept, there's no reason to spend eons on execution. The resulting work won't communicate anything past its surface attributes. The best illustration work conveys an idea artfully, while leaving traces of the artist's hand clearly visible in the work. Otherwise, what is there for the audience to connect with?

Take part in the following challenge, and seek the human element in a piece of conceptual illustration.

> *"The real fight is about what should be in the marketplace and what should not. Should education be a marketable commodity? Should health care?"*
>
> —Susan George

CHALLENGE

You've been commissioned to draw three spot illustrations for an upcoming magazine article about the new movement toward membership-based, flat-fee health care clinics. In the case of the clinic being featured in this piece, they charge fifty dollars a year for unlimited visits during business hours, and your cost per visit is only twenty dollars—with no appointment required and only a brief wait to meet with a doctor.

The art director wants you to make the illustrations look "low cost but very high quality," to support the idea in the article that inexpensive does not necessarily mean cheap.

If you've never done conceptual illustration work for a magazine, this challenge should be a treat. Be sure to focus in on the ideas first to ensure that they are solid before you start producing the final product.

TAKE IT FURTHER

Lay out the article in the magazine with the illustrations in place. How can the illustration style be extended into the type choice and used through the entire piece?

1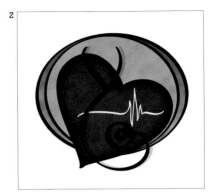

2

3

1,2,3 Designer and illustrator Lisa Stewart, after completing this challenge, noted that "this new movement [in affordable health care] requires an understanding of the general level of care offered at these clinics. Quality service [should be] reflected with sophisticated imagery, augmenting the presentation for overall well-being and contentment… The sophisticated calligraphic linework reflects the level of sophisticated services… Friendly, color-coded images promote basic mnemonic assistance for non-English-speaking consumers… Beyond the membership article, the imagery can be utilized within the care clinic as signage as well as additional print and web collateral."

4 Your brief wait for treatment should be just as simple as turning and opening a pill bottle. This simple hand-rendered illustration is from a series by designer Jake Rae.

4

Paper, Plastic, Glass, Vapor

 120 minutes Research

72

A large percentage of the human body is made of water. Over seventy percent of the Earth's surface is covered by water. In most nations, access to clean drinking water has only increased. Safe, clean tap water continues to flow in more than a billion homes worldwide.

Yet if we look just twenty years into the future, the forecast is cloudy. With the lack of potable water for hygiene, as well as heavy consumption of freshwater by agriculture and industry, many countries are seeing the potential for long-term risks to their citizens. The long-term fear is that we'll be drowning in scarcity, especially with the reduction of fresh water in icecaps and glaciers melting due to climate change.

In this challenge, you'll need to take an ethical stance regarding our society's long-term access to fresh water—and back your decision with a well-designed rationale.

> *"I think it's going to be quite hard to make an impact [as a designer] if your aim is to improve people's quality of life by producing aesthetically pleasing graphics alone. If you see your purpose as communicating a message, then you've got to have something to say. This inevitably means you have a perspective, which does make [design] a political activity."*
>
> —Delyth Morgan, "Politics" (from *Good: An Introduction to Ethics in Graphic Design* by Lucienne Roberts)

CHALLENGE

A client contacts you with a novel proposition: Help them create the overall brand position, market strategy and packaging for a new bottled water that is likely to be sourced from the Antarctic. Would you take on the project?

If your answer is yes, clearly describe how would you name and bottle the project, considering its overall environmental impact.

If your answer is no, recommend an alternative solution.

No matter which answer you provide, your final deliverable for this challenge is a polished one-sheet, complete with infographics, that will persuade your client to accept your recommendation.

TAKE IT FURTHER

Based on your recommendation, further help your client by crafting a "vision document" that they can provide to investors to help raise venture capital.

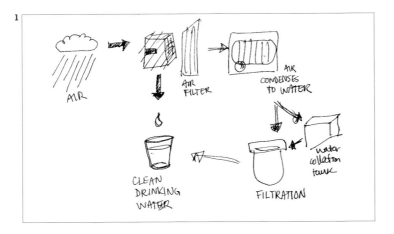

1,2 Katharine Widdows decided not to draw water for consumption from the Antarctic/Arctic regions. She then researched alternative technologies that wouldn't rely on extracting water directly from fragile ecosystems and created a one-sheet for atmospheric water generators (AWGs), which "extract moisture from the atmosphere through a condensation process and transform it into absolutely pure, healthy drinking water."

airwater

Wondering about the future of water?

The world's supply of fresh water from streams, rivers, lakes, and rainfall is in danger. Scientists are predicting that some regions may experience increases in precipitation and run-off while other regions may experience decreases. Changes in sustainable water availability could have considerable regional-scale consequences for economies as well as ecosystems.

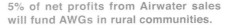

Airwater can be created anywhere on the planet.

Why wait for this impending crisis to unfold? Technology already exists to transcend this problem. Atmospheric Water Generators (AWG) extract moisture from the atmosphere through a condensation process and transform it into absolutely pure, healthy drinking water.

AWGs work by drawing air from the atmosphere into a very cold space, wherein the vapour is transformed into a condensate (water) due to heat exchange, just as it does in a natural rainfall. The unit also acts as an effective dehumidifier and air purifier.

5% of net profits from Airwater sales will fund AWGs in rural communities.

THE JALIMUDI VILLAGE PROJECT

The villagers of Jalimudi, a small village in Andhra Pradesh, are getting water from the air thanks to modern day technology. Jalimudi is the first village in the world to have a sustained water supply that is not from the sea, river, lake, pipeline or borewell, or transported by water tankers and trucks.

884 million people do not have access to clean water. Many rural communities use a system of collecting dew or resort to walking long distances for drinking water; however, often these water supplies are contaminated, carrying water born diseases that can make people sick or even die. AWGs can solve the problem.

On average, one person uses 166 disposable plastic water bottles per year.

For further information visit: http://www.airwatercorp.com

We'll bottle it in earth-friendly, returnable glass.

· 8 out of 10 plastic water bottles used in the United States become garbage or end up in a landfill.

· on average, one person uses 166 disposable plastic water bottles a year.

· composed of a polycarbonate plastic, water bottles have a molecular makeup that allows for a dioxin to leach into any liquid it holds.

· Glass containers are 100 percent recyclable, can be recycled endlessly and recovered glass is used as the majority ingredient in new glass containers.

· An estimated 80 percent of recovered glass containers are made into new glass bottles.

· 34.5 percent of glass beer and soft drink bottles and 28.1 percent of all glass containers were recycled in 2007.

3

fresh...local...unique

Locally sourced water infused with: Electrolytes, Essences, Vitamins, and/or Caffeine...fresh...local...unique

What is Sorce?
Sorce is a revolutionary new way of distributing fresh, clean, local water to the masses via conveniently placed vending machines.

Who will use Sorce vending machines?
Anyone and everyone who is sick of having to rely on bottled water due to convenience and portability as well as those wanting to reduce their environmental foot print.

Will consumers need to use their own bottles?
Consumers will have the choice to use their own bottle or purchase a reusable and trendy canteen style bottle from the vending machine.

What kinds of water come from the machines?
Consumers will have plenty of options when it comes to their uniquely styled water choices. They can choose from chilled/room temperature water and then add or omit electrolytes, herbal/fruit essences, vitamins and/or caffeine. What they get is a water choice that rivals other flavored and unflavored bottled waters on the market.

How much will Sorce water cost?
Public water costs will be averaged per ounce in addition to a small fee to assist in the cost of maintenance and stocking of the machines. Roughly $.50 for 16oz of water(unflavored), $.10 per option(essences, etc.) and $.65 per sorce bottle if needed. Total cost will rival most artesian bottled waters on the market as well as some public water source bottled waters such as Nestle, Aquafina, etc.

What information will be on the machines?
Every vending machine will include an informational plaque on the side displaying a map with the location of the water source for that particular machine as well as the nutritional values of the infusion ingredients. Facts about bottled water could also be displayed if desired.

WOULD YOU LIKE TO GET INVOLVED? Contact us!
Jane Doe
Sorce Inc.
1412 11th Ave E
Seattle, WA 98102

tel/ 206.344.4566
jane@sorce.com
web/ www.sorce.com

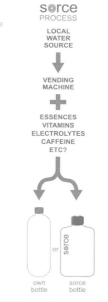

VENDING MACHINE
SIDE VIEW

Map displays location of water source as well as nutritional facts for "infused" water

sorce PROCESS

LOCAL WATER SOURCE

VENDING MACHINE

ESSENCES VITAMINS ELECTROLYTES CAFFEINE ETC?

own bottle · or · sorce bottle

BOTTLED WATER / facts
- The amount of carbon dioxide emitted annually during the transportation to California of bottled water from France, Italy and Fiji accounts for an estimated 9,700 tons of carbon dioxide, the equivalent of the yearly emissions from 1,700 cars on the road.
- Millions of consumers go with it because of the portability and convenience.
- More than 40% of all bottled water is tap water
- Public water supply is more stringently regulated (by the Environmental Protection Agency) than bottled water (by the Food and Drug Administration)

3 In the process of wrestling with this challenge, designer Jessica Thrasher came up with the idea for Sorce, "Locally sourced water infused with electrolytes, essences, vitamins and/or caffeine… Anyone who is sick of having to rely on bottled water due to convenience and portability as well as those wanting to reduce their environmental footprint… will have the choice to use their own bottle or purchase a reusable and trendy canteen-style bottle from the vending machine. At the machine, consumers can choose from chilled/room-temperature water and then add or omit electrolytes, herbal/fruit essences, vitamins and/or caffeine. What they get is a water choice that rivals other flavored and unflavored bottled waters on the market… Every vending machine will include an informational plaque on the side displaying a map with the location of the water source for that particular machine as well as the nutritional values of the infusion ingredients. Facts about bottled water could also be displayed, if desired."

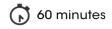

73 Free Tibet Blog

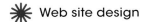

⏱ 60 minutes   ✳ Web site design

Remember the glory days, when a solid brochure-ware web site was the cost of entry for success in the Internet age?

The days of the static web site, laden with bland descriptions of your products and services, have been replaced by living conversations. Nowadays, a single Google search can bring you to the doorstep of practically any thought leader or media guru, alive or dead. Their blogs and Twitter feeds dispense all sorts of free wisdom and advice. Many of them hope to foster and spread their ideas, and in return, they'll receive input and collaboration around how those ideas can be advanced.

But even with high-quality blogging systems, it takes a designer's deft hand to make an impact in a cluttered online space. Otherwise, what you're saying may be lost in the visual noise of Blog Template #487, "Stripes and Shadows."

When it comes to blog design, this challenge will push you to transcend the ordinary.

> *"There is no need for temples, no need for complicated philosophies. My brain and my heart are my temples; my philosophy is kindness."*
>
> —The Dalai Lama

CHALLENGE

The Dalai Lama is well represented on Facebook, but what he really needs is his own blog. The problem is, there are dozens of "unofficial" blogs out there that could be confused with the musings of His Holiness.

How can you differentiate the Dalai Lama's blog experience? What content would make it the most meaningful for frequent visitors? Would you seek up-to-the-moment updates, or weave together material from his many books, lectures and teachings in order to explain his beliefs? And most importantly, what kind of communication would you want to foster between the Dalai Lama and his readership, and how would it be visually represented?

TAKE IT FURTHER

Based on your overall design strategy, consider how to localize this new blog for the Dalai Lama's world-wide audience.

1,2 Designer and illustrator Nicholas Nawroth used elements associated with the Dalai Lama to design his web site. "I started out by doing some research on the Dalai Lama's current official web site as well as a couple of books I have in my library. I also looked at some of the other Tibet-related blogs. I then developed my criteria for what the Dalai Lama's official blog should include: the colors yellow, red, black; the typeface Trajan Pro (which is used on his official web site); and it should be clean, simple and convey happiness… I decided to add a hand-drawn sun and moon (I saw them on the Dalai Lama's official web site) to balance out the header. My final touch was to add a bit of texture to the background to tie the whole page together and complete the hand-made aspect of the layout."

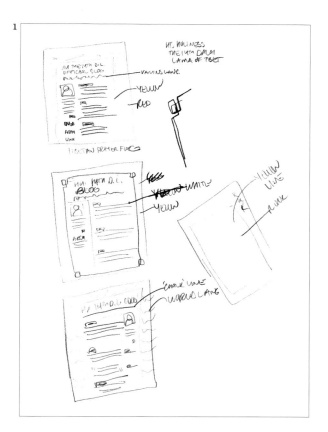

3 Jon Bell at frog design and I timeboxed ourselves for 17 minutes and came up with ideas for this challenge. We settled upon the notion of having a horizontal navigation that you could use to move through the wisdom of the various incarnations of the Dalai Lama. The page would then filter to show the appropriate entries. I took 10 minutes after that ideation to put together this rough sketch, implying the ways in which conversations could happen through time in the blog. The main visual motif that would tie the layout together is the bodhi tree—some of which take up to 3,000 years to fully mature.

4 Thinking about the wit exhibited by His Holiness, Donnie Dinch's approach to this challenge was to propose the "Daily Dose of the Dalai Lama," with tweet-sized bites of text that express what's on his mind.

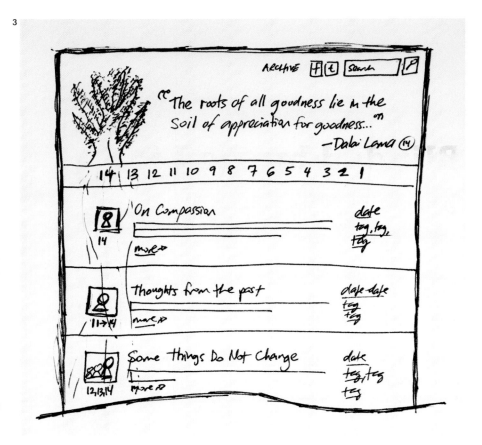

Blinded by the Light

 120 minutes   Design research, product design

Designing for disability requires great empathy and a willingness to dive wholesale into the worldview of your audience through deep research and observation. Yes, you can tie a blindfold over your eyes and experience what it's like to be visually impaired. But your sojourn is but a brief interlude compared to the difficulties of living in a world crafted for those who can see. Those with visual impairment have little context for the way we've constructed our communities. They construct their own systems for navigating the world, and as a result, they have unique problems that can be solved—by design.

In the following challenge, use your powers of design thinking to help solve a common problem that has unique considerations for those lacking sight.

> **"There is a condition worse than blindness, and that is, seeing something that isn't there."**
>
> —Thomas Hardy

CHALLENGE

Invent a method for blind people to discern when they've been in the sun too long, thereby helping reduce their risk of sunburn and skin cancer.

Is it through education? A product? Adapting a piece of technology they already use? Who will tell them about your solution, and how will they adopt it?

Be aware that no matter what solution you choose, you'll need to execute it in a manner that will be consumable by the appropriate audiences. As an example: If you're going to provide educational outreach tools for doctors to use during patient visits, you could design a brochure with both visual text and Braille. But if you're going to reach out directly to visually impaired people via the Internet, you will need to be aware of how they're going to consume your design solution through that medium.

TAKE IT FURTHER

Would your design solution still function if you were to provide it to someone who is both visually impaired and deaf? Would it be possible to adapt your solution for those who cannot hear as well?

1,2,3 I gave this challenge to my Spring 2009 class, but told them to spend their first hour of brainstorming starting to understand emotionally what it's like to be visually impaired. We walked over to the Olympic Sculpture Park in downtown Seattle, where two students tied cloths over their eyes and spent half an hour being questioned by the class regarding how it felt to be out in the sun on a hot day.

Out of that initial brainstorm, the group gravitated toward creating a physical product that could be used by blind people without requiring that they carry around an extra object all day. This prototype for Sunsmart was the result—solar alert sunglasses for the blind.

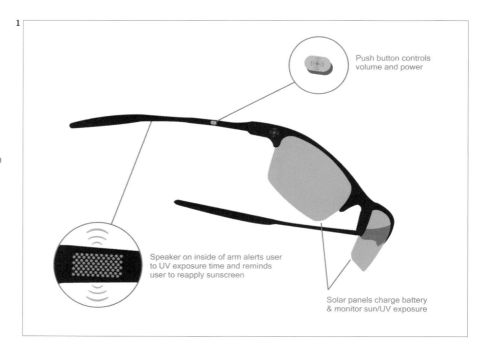

1

Push button controls volume and power

Speaker on inside of arm alerts user to UV exposure time and reminds user to reapply sunscreen

Solar panels charge battery & monitor sun/UV exposure

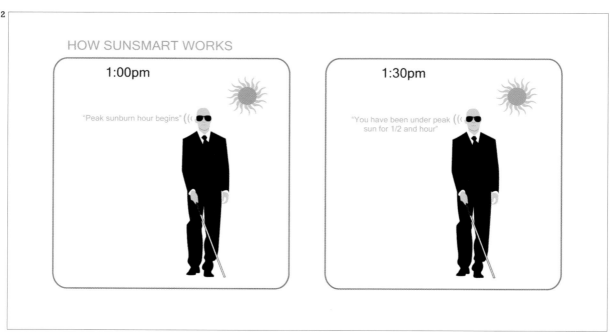

2

HOW SUNSMART WORKS

1:00pm

"Peak sunburn hour begins"

1:30pm

"You have been under peak sun for 1/2 and hour"

3

Sunsmart
solar alert sunglasses for the blind

The inability to visually monitor the condition of one's skin can be dangerous. The blind need to be able to enjoy the sun and also be aware of when they have had too much sun exposure. Over exposure to the sun can cause sun burn and eventually lead to skin cancer. With sun exposure awareness on the rise, it's time to give the blind an option that makes their lives easier and more enjoyable.

SUNSMART sunglasses give the blind a new and easy way to assess their sun damage risk by alerting them to the rate of UV exposure as well as offering a friendly reminder to seek shade or reapply sunscreen.

FACTS:

- Visually impaired and blind people have devised a number of techniques that allow them to complete daily activities using their remaining senses.

- Many people with serious visual impairments can travel independently, using a wide range of tools and techniques.

- People may use talking thermometers, enlarged oven dials, talking watches, talking clocks, talking scales, talking calculators, talking compasses and other talking equipment.

WOULD YOU LIKE TO GET INVOLVED? Contact us!

Jane Doe
Sorce Inc.   tel/ 206.344.4566
1412 11th Ave E   jane@sorce.com
Seattle, WA 98102   web/ www.sorce.com

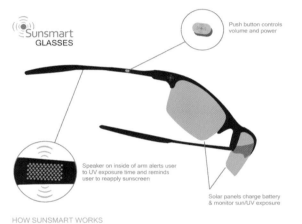

Sunsmart GLASSES

Push button controls volume and power

Speaker on inside of arm alerts user to UV exposure time and reminds user to reapply sunscreen

Solar panels charge battery & monitor sun/UV exposure

HOW SUNSMART WORKS

1:00pm
"Peak sunburn hour begins"

1:30pm
"You have been under peak sun for 1/2 and hour"

Touch Screen of Deaf Rock

 120 minutes Interaction storyboarding, exhibit design

I live near the Experience Music Project, a museum in Seattle dedicated to rock music from Chuck Berry to Jimi Hendrix to Sleater-Kinney. One of the most amazing exhibits in the museum is a sound laboratory. Want to learn how to play bass? The frets light up, helping teach you the notes. How about the drums? A full kit, wired up with robotic arms, will guide you through the rudiments of a funky beat.

Spending a few hours in this exhibit will fulfill the dreams of any tone-deaf rock aficionado who's wanted to play a hot lick from a Rolling Stones tune or sing along with a synth-laden track by the Eurythmics. (And I've spent many an hour there jamming out "Louie Louie" on the guitar.) But the last time I was there, I realized that enjoying the exhibit was contingent on one specific thing: the ability to hear.

So, in the following challenge, bring music to those ears that *can't* hear.

> *"Hearing is a form of touch. I hear it through the body, by opening myself up. Sometimes it almost hits you in the face."*
>
> —Evelyn Glennie, a profoundly deaf Scottish solo percussionist

 CHALLENGE

Create a novel exhibit experience at your local children's museum that lets deaf people feel different kinds of music. The exhibit should also accommodate hearing children and parents who want to understand what it's like to experience different kinds of music physically, not aurally.

What kinds of music would you want to share with these audiences? How would you prompt deaf children to interact with the exhibit? What technology would you use to manifest sound physically?

TAKE IT FURTHER

Find a friend to help you create a paper prototype at the size of the actual exhibit experience. Then test it in a walkthrough and see how your ideas can be improved with their feedback.

1

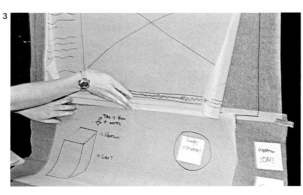

2

3

4

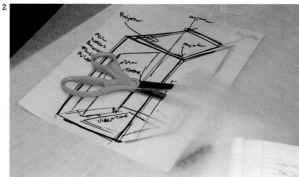

5

6

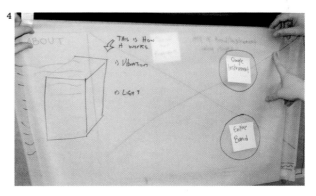

1,2 Mark Notermann, Meg Doyle, Claire Kohler and Donnie Dinch tried this exercise as a team, designing and refining their initial interaction ideas through a paper prototyping exercise. After forty-five minutes, I attempted to use the interface without any aural input, then the team clarified various features of their exhibit based on the feedback.

3,4 This is the first screen of the interface. When you walk in, instructions describe what will happen when you use the exhibit, and prompt you to choose a single instrument or a style of music. Once you've made a choice, this screen doesn't appear again unless you hit the "start over" or "back" button on the exhibit interface. Using tracing paper makes it easy to swap screens in and out and quickly revise interface elements.

5,6 The user sees footprints on the floor. If they stand there, vibrations from the music will carry up through their legs. The users are prompted

to "feel the music" by putting their hands on the handprints. The entire surface may be vibrating, but the visual cues will draw the user to start here.

7,8 The main exhibit interface has a large video player with a scrub bar so you can see the progress of the video. To the left of the video is an "about" panel with text that describes the music or instrument being played. Donnie and I dis-cussed the usability considerations about reading long-form text in touch screen interfaces. How could the user easily scroll the text with-out a mouse? Should you use your hand to scroll the text up and down by touching the screen and drag-ging the text downward? That would obstruct a portion of the screen with your arm, blocking out content. However, if there's an arrow at the bottom of the screen, content won't be covered and you won't strain your arm by reaching up to keep moving text.

7

8

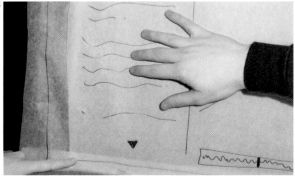

9

10

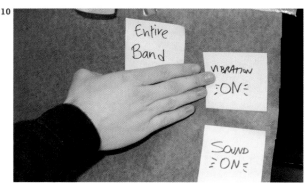

9 The first version of the interface had a large box that overtook more than half of the exhibit screen. This box contained either single instruments or styles of music. In the next revision of this part of the interface, the buttons were collapsed into a menu that was at the bottom of the screen.

10 What if you aren't deaf? What if you don't want to feel the vibration? In the end, we added on/off toggles for the vibration and audio, as it's likely that a mixture of deaf and non-deaf people will play with the exhibit.

11 After the class, Claire Kohler visualized what the exhibit could look like. LED lights glow and pulse, pointing the exhibit visitors toward use of the touchscreen interface. The walls could also vary in color, texture and pattern in time to the music.

11

Sniff Test

 90 minutes   ✳ Exhibit design

Walking through a department store is olfactory assault and battery. Here, place this sample of Di Patchouli #8 on your wrist, inhale deeply and then go scrub your arm for a good half hour to rid yourself of the scent memory.

It can be difficult to think clearly when your nose is provoked by manufactured scents. And an unpleasant aroma provides us with such visceral emotional feedback that any encounter outside our range of comfort can be completely overwhelming.

Most designers I know are perfectly comfortable with manipulating visual, tactile and auditory feedback to create compelling brand experiences. But when it comes to managing a person's sense of smell, all bets are off.

In the following challenge, see how you can use your design prowess to create a scent-focused museum experience that won't stink for everyone involved.

> ## "I would rather smell of nothing than of perfume."
> —Marcus Aurelius, Roman emperor

CHALLENGE

Create an exhibit at the Smithsonian Institution's National Museum of Natural History about the history of perfume. It is critical that each exhibit participant be able to sample and smell various perfumes in a non-wasteful manner.

Think of a way to control the experience by design so museum visitors won't be overwhelmed by too many scents in the exhibit environment.

TAKE IT FURTHER

Name and brand the exhibit, then determine how you'd advertise it—both in print ads and in a guerrilla experience that takes your exhibit idea into the real world.

1,2,3,4 As part of an in-class brain-storm, Jessica Thrasher, Katherine Widdows, Michelle Cormack and Shimon Alkon created prototypes of colorfully designed masks that museum patrons could borrow for their journey through the scent exhibit. The design of the masks would vary in size and shape, mimicking both human noses and the noses of various animals—such as the toucan shown here. Jessica then took the class brainstorm notes and sketched out her vision of how the exhibit design could integrate with the masks.

1
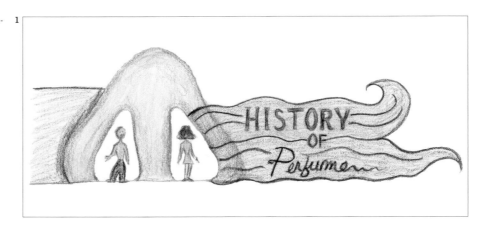

2

3
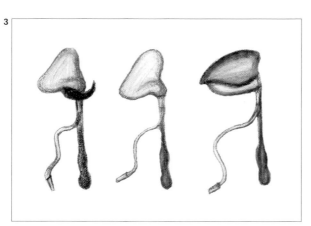

4

Can You Hear Me Now?

 90 minutes  TV commercials

I remember visiting my grandmother on Sunday afternoons when I was a child. While sitting on the couch in her Baltimore apartment and munching away at sugar-free raspberry thumbprint cookies, the television would always be switched on—with the sound off—to keep her company.

As visuals for varying products interwove with golf tournaments and travel programs, I noticed the importance of sound as part of a broadcast advertising message. Happy men in their fifties and sixties were silently singing the praises of prescription drugs via bold italic sans-serif type. Ed McMahon hawked participation in a multimillion-dollar sweepstakes. Most of those mid-afternoon commercials were intelligently constructed to work entirely as visuals, for the hearing impaired. (And vice versa: If you only heard what they were saying, the message would still be conveyed.)

In the following challenge, you'll find ways to convey a powerful television spot without sound. But unlike the examples I noted above, the lack of music or voiceover in your commercial is critical to the message's conceit.

TAKE IT FURTHER

Is your concept strong enough to be communicated in any medium? See if you can translate your spot into print advertising, billboards, radio, or a guerrilla-marketing campaign for the target audience.

CHALLENGE

Create storyboards for a thirty-second TV spot advertising an adoption service that specializes in locating parents for deaf children. The spot may have no sound or voiceover whatsoever, only on-screen text and visuals, plus a title card. As part of your storyboards, you will need to devise a name and mark for the adoption service.

"If you're trying to persuade people to do something, or buy something, it seems to me you should use their language, the language they use every day, the language in which they think."

—David Ogilvy

1

or someone
who can't hear
the words
I love yo

Frame 1

Frame 2

It doesn't take much
to see
love

Frame 3

Frame 4

Frame 5

It doesn't take much
to feel
love

Frame 6

1 Michael Anthony, a Buffalo-based designer, solved this challenge with the following twelve-frame storyboard for *Signs of Love*.

Frame 1 (Open to off-white screen soft-focus, some blurred figures in the far distance… At the same time, sound effects of a pleasant conversation that is muffled and distant, such as a profoundly deaf person might hear. Sound trails off quickly. No voiceover. There is no sound again until the final frame.)

Text comes into focus from the distance, then moves across the screen right to left, in fragments, each at its own medium slow pace:

"For someone who can't hear the words 'I love you'…"

Frame 2 Visual: Indoor medium/ tight shot of a mother—soft daylight all around. She is reading from a children's book while projecting a gentle and playful attitude. We don't see the child yet.

Frame 3 Text again moves across the screen right to left: "It doesn't take much to see love."

Frame 4 Visual: Cut to tight shot of the child responding—a naturally charming giggle, not too intense, they are sharing a bonding moment. (We see the child has a hearing aid.)

Visual: Pull back to reveal both mother and child lying on their tummies or sitting at a small desk sharing the book.

Frame 5 Visual: Full shot from a distance, father and child (approx. six years old). Soft daylight outdoors. Maybe along a shore or at a kids' sporting event. Interaction: Father and child are playing; during the action, dad signs and speaks. The child smiles and laughs.

Frame 6 Text again moves across the screen right to left: "It doesn't take much to feel love."

Exercise 77

Frame 7

Frame 8

Frame 9

Frame 10

ake much
to make a child
with special nee
feel s

Frame 11

Signs of Love
adoption services devoted to deaf children

Frame 12

Frame 7 Visual: Cut to tight shot of their hands; the big hand gives the little hand a soft loving squeeze. Wait a beat… The child's hand squeezes back.

Frame 8 Text again moves across the screen right to left: "It doesn't take much to taste love."

Frame 9 Visual: Full shot of an ethnic family in a middle-class kitchen around the dinner table, sharing a warm moment and meal. Mother, father, sister (around age nine) and child (boy or girl around age five, with hearing aid). One person may use sign language and speak at the same time, clearly telling a funny story to all.

Frame 10 Visual: Child's bedroom, medium shot of toddler in printed footie pajamas from behind as she runs into the arms of her parent. The parent scoops up the child, crossing her arms over the child's back to embrace her, making the international sign for love.

Frame 11 Text again moves across the screen right to left: "It doesn't take much to make a child with special needs… feel special."

Sound effects: Sound comes back up muffled. We hear a "mmm"

sound that people make when hugging.

Frame 12 Voiceover: "Just a simple 'sign of love.'"

Visual: The parent-and-child hug dissolves into the logo that is in the same spot on the screen. Insert contact info.

# **Bending Geography**

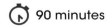 

🕐 90 minutes ✳ Information design

"Not to scale. Some detail has been omitted." And that's how it should be.

Not all maps must precisely render exact street locations in perfect scale and proportion to be useful to readers. In fact, as information designer William Bardel points out, distortion and detail omission is often used to produce better maps. Bending geography can enhance legibility and improve findability for specific uses. For example, most New York City transit maps show the island of Manhattan much wider than it actually is to add space for complex route labeling. Yet this distortion doesn't seem to bother commuters. Maps can be stunning examples of information design that are as much art as pieces of functional utility.

Interested in trying your hand at making one of these maps? Take on the following challenge by William, which will have you bending the geography of where you live.

> **"The virtue of maps, they show what can be done with limited space, they foresee that everything can happen therein."**
>
> —José Saramago, *The Stone Raft*

CHALLENGE

Find a map of your town, city or neighborhood and see how much you can remove from it (such as secondary streets) and how much you can abstract features such as parks, rivers, roads and train tracks by using simple geometric forms: squares, rectangles, triangles, circles and simple lines.

Can you accomplish this without your map losing its recognition and function for navigation? What does the result look like? You may be surprised how beautiful your town, city or neighborhood looks in a simplified graphic form.

TAKE IT FURTHER

What if you push your design even further, to a higher level of abstraction? See what new design opportunities suggest themselves.

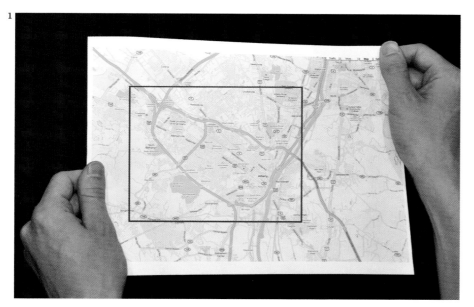

1,2,3 William Bardel says, "Start by studying reference materials to identify major roadways, parks, natural features and key building footprints. Create a draft sketch and then modify by smoothing out lines and replacing real-world shapes with geometric ones. The key to simplified maps is to start with major features and work your way down to smaller ones. Average your lines between their real locations, and those that conform to basic geometric proportions."

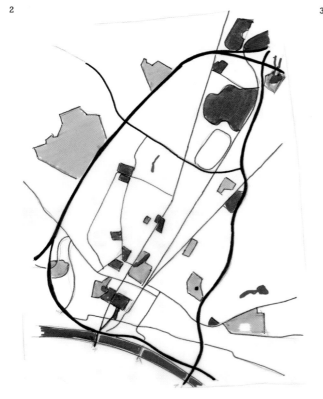

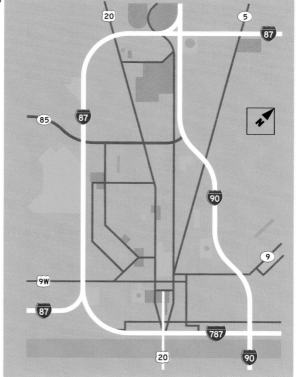

4

4,5 This is an icon map of Rome on dinnerware. Joel Katz's *Urban Icons* project "was inspired by a visit to the museum under the parvis of Notre-Dame in Paris in about 1990, which modeled the earliest Paris: a roughly circular wall; in the middle of which the arc of a river; in the middle of the river an island; in the middle of the island a church. What could be simpler or more iconic? The very blueprint of the concept of a city.

"So was born the notion of re-mapping cities (which I have always loved) in circles (which I have always loved)—sun, moon, earth, plates. I imagined a dinner party with each place setting a different city, and myself as the Joel Chicago of urban plans. I set myself some objectives and some constraints: They would be geometric, and axial or radial or con-centric, but in any case 'organized,' as so many cities, whether planned or unplanned, are; while taking enormous liberties with geography, relationships would be relatively true. A vocabulary of icons began to emerge—stars for museums, crosses for churches—as did the cities—Philadelphia, London, Rome, Paris (complete), Kyoto, Bruges, Venice, Florence, Siena, Barcelona."

5

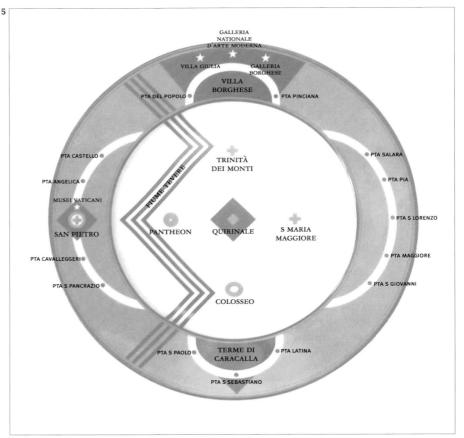

What Do I Know?

 120 minutes   User interface design, research

Remember using the *Encyclopedia Britannica* and the *Oxford English Dictionary*? These hefty tomes were once considered static repositories of the "final word" on history, language use and modern culture. They have been supplanted by ever-evolving online resources such as Wikipedia. Communal wikis now provide human-curated content that is more relevant than most other knowledge resources. If you have a question about anything knowledge-related, an answer is probably somewhere on Wikipedia. (Including the *OED*'s definition of the word "knowledge"—in the entry on knowledge.)

People also send out queries for information to human networks, such as those that exist on Twitter and Facebook. In a few minutes, you can probe the knowledge or opinions of your followers and get an almost instant response without having to seek out that information yourself via search engines. This is a kind of information acquisition enabled by technology that had never existed before—what we now call the lazyweb—that leverages our collective knowledge as people.

> *"I have a dream for the web [in which computers] become capable of analyzing all the data on the web—the content, links and transactions between people and computers. A 'Semantic Web,' which should make this possible, has yet to emerge, but when it does, the day-to-day mechanisms of trade, bureaucracy and our daily lives will be handled by machines talking to machines ."*
>
> —Tim Berners-Lee, inventor of the World Wide Web, 1999

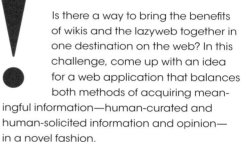

CHALLENGE

Is there a way to bring the benefits of wikis and the lazyweb together in one destination on the web? In this challenge, come up with an idea for a web application that balances both methods of acquiring meaningful information—human-curated and human-solicited information and opinion—in a novel fashion.

Here are some questions you'll need to answer along the way: What mechanisms are in place to ensure that the provided information is accurate? When querying a topic, will you need results that reference facts, opinions or both? And the thorniest question of all: What kind of knowledge do you want your web app to provide users—and will it evolve over time to understand our needs?

TAKE IT FURTHER

Once you've devised your idea and checked the Internet to see if it's already been made, try designing the user interface.

You may not be able to come up with a feasible solution for this challenge in the time allotted. Countless designers, scientists and philosophers from antiquity to present have struggled with the ideas presented here. But do not fear—even two hours spent thinking about this problem may provide you with surprising insights and a new point of view on the stated problem.

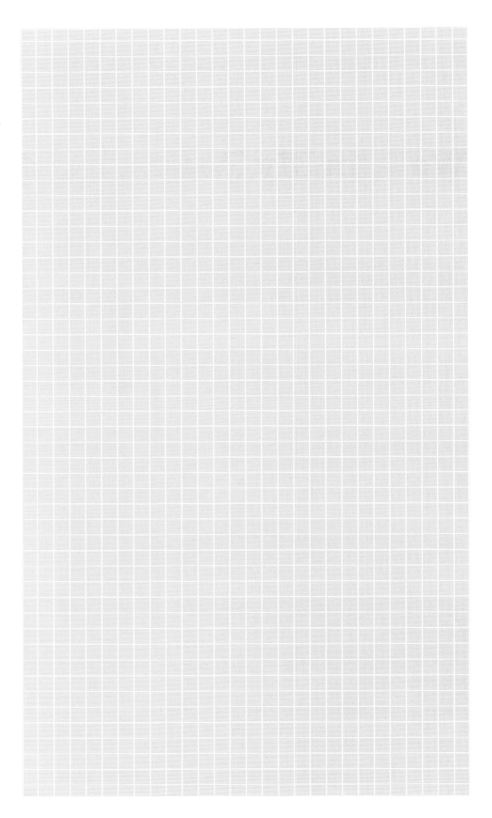

Well, in My Book...

 60 minutes  Book design

I can't count how many people I've met, especially designers, who say that they "don't have a book in them." I couldn't disagree more.

My home is crammed full of books of all shapes and sizes. Since an early age, I've spent at least an hour every day curled up with thought-provoking reads. And if there's one thing I've discovered from my devotion to the written word, it's that we have an infinite capacity for learning from other people's experience.

Endless blog posts and conversations online may provide us with information and insight, but the art-fueled moments that strike deep into our hearts more frequently occur when we delve into books. So, with this final challenge, use your design talent to share with the world your irreplaceable point of view.

CHALLENGE

Design a book that highlights what you've discovered over the course of your life. Use the time limit to write the outline of your book, and to decide what kinds of material it will contain. Then, while you're designing the book, think about how you will provide readers with a view into how you see the world—both in your copy and your choice of illustration style.

"Regretting my past keeps me from moving on."

—Hyun-Jung Hwang, in response to Stefan Sagmeister's *Things I Have Learned in My Life So Far*

TAKE IT FURTHER

Now that you've finished your book, think outside it. Could this also be a stand-up calendar for your desk? An animated screensaver for your computer? A digital billboard on the street outside your home? How can you share what you have learned with the world?

6

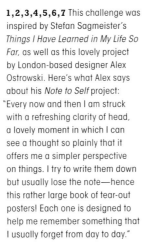

1,2,3,4,5,6,7 This challenge was inspired by Stefan Sagmeister's *Things I Have Learned in My Life So Far*, as well as this lovely project by London-based designer Alex Ostrowski. Here's what Alex says about his *Note to Self* project: "Every now and then I am struck with a refreshing clarity of head, a lovely moment in which I can see a thought so plainly that it offers me a simpler perspective on things. I try to write them down but usually lose the note—hence this rather large book of tear-out posters! Each one is designed to help me remember something that I usually forget from day to day."

7

Acknowledgments

A good number of people have devoted thousands of hours collectively to this project, and I must thank them here.

The largest thank-you goes to my wife, Mary Paynter Sherwin. She was a substantive collaborator with me—from the first glimmerings of this project, to brainstorming the actual challenges, to helping me edit, proof and source quotes for the text of the book. Her name should really be on the spine next to mine.

This book would never have been possible without the participation of the nine students that partook of my "80 Works for Designers" seminars through 2009, both at the Creative Academy at Seattle Central Community College and as a class held at Worktank Brand Storytellers. My students road-tested almost every challenge in this volume, with good spirits and only minor grumbling, and their conceptual work illustrates a good portion of this volume. They are: Shimon Alkon, Michelle Cormack, Donnie Dinch, Meg Doyle, Claire Kohler, Mark Notermann, Jake Rae, Jessica Thrasher and Katharine Widdows. Katharine Widdows deserves the gold star as being the only student to provide complete solutions for all eighty challenges, through hell or high water. Mark Notermann also warrants attention for his boundless creativity and tenacity, which served as inspiration for everyone involved.

All of the working and student designers who solved challenges for this book deserve praise. Much of their work is within these pages, and what I couldn't squeeze in here I will share on the Creative Workshop web site (www.CreativeWorkshopTheBook.com).

The research for this book was initially conducted via a survey that I sent out to a number of working designers, creative directors and studio principals. Special thanks to Carrie Byrne, David Conrad, Duane King, Jon Lindstrand, Wendy Quesinberry, Andy Rutledge, Daniel Schutzsmith and Michel Vrana for taking part and helping to guide this project.

I have to single out for special thanks the following people: Jill Vartenigian and Marc Salverda of the Creative Academy at Seattle Central Community College, who supported me in teaching the first incarnation of this text in their program; Scott Scheff, who co-taught one of my classes and contributed ideas that wended their way into a number of challenges; Melinda Partin and Leslie Rugaber at Worktank Brand Storytellers, who provided me ample time and space at the office to teach; Dave Fletcher of theMechanism, who graciously agreed to take on extra projects and help me find designers for the more difficult challenges; my friends and colleagues at frog design, who road-tested a number of the challenges involving physical prototyping and provided ongoing encouragement throughout the publication process; and all of my family and friends who have supported this project from the beginning.

A special thank you also goes out to Megan Patrick at HOW Books, who saw the shape of this book in a brief post I'd included on my blog, ChangeOrder: Business + Process of Design. And to my editor, Amy Schell Owen, who helped me shape the material into the book you see here today.

Resources

Adams, Sean, Noreen Morioka, and Terry Stone. *Logo Design Workbook: A Hands-On Guide to Creating Logos*. Gloucester, Mass.: Rockport Publishers, 2004.

Barry, Pete. *The Advertising Concept Book*. London: Thames & Hudson, 2008.

Bly, Robert W. *The Copywriter's Handbook: A Step-By-Step Guide to Writing Copy That Sells*. 3rd ed. New York: Henry Holt, 2005.

Bringhurst, Robert. *The Elements of Typographic Style*. 3rd ed. Point Roberts, Wash.: Hartley & Marks, Publishers, 2004.

Cooper, Alan, Robert Reimann and David Cronin. *About Face 3: The Essentials of Interaction Design*. Indianapolis: Wiley Publishing, 2007.

de Bono, Edward. *Six Thinking Hats*. Boston: Back Bay Books, 1999.

Donaldson, Timothy. *Shapes for Sounds*. New York: Mark Batty Publisher, 2008.

Dougher, Sarah and Josh Berger. *100 Habits of Successful Graphic Designers: Insider Secrets on Working Smart and Staying Creative*. Gloucester, Mass.: Rockport Publishers, 2003.

Elam, Kimberly. *Grid Systems: Principles of Organizing Type*. New York: Princeton Architectural Press, 2004.

Fletcher, Alan. *The Art of Looking Sideways*. London: Phaidon, 2001.

Garrett, Jesse James. *The Elements of User Experience: User-Centered Design for the Web*. Indianapolis: New Riders, 2002.

Gibson, David. *The Wayfinding Handbook: Information Design for Public Places*. New York: Princeton Architectural Press, 2009.

Harrison, Sam. *IdeaSpotting: How to Find Your Next Great Idea*. Cincinnati: HOW Books, 2006.

Lidwell, William, Kritina Holden and Jill Butler. *Universal Principles of Design*. Beverly, Mass.: Rockport Publishers, 2003.

Lupton, Ellen. *Thinking With Type: A Critical Guide for Designers, Writers, Editors, & Students*. New York: Princeton Architectural Press, 2004.

MacKenzie, Gordon. *Orbiting the Giant Hairball: A Corporate Fool's Guide to Surviving With Grace*. New York: Viking, 1998.

McAlhone, Beryl and David Stuart. *A Smile in the Mind: Witty Thinking in Graphic Design*. London: Phaidon, 1998.

Meggs, Philip B. and Alston W. Purvis. *Meggs' History of Graphic Design*. 4th ed. Hoboken, N.J.: John Wiley & Sons, 2006.

Michalko, Michael. *Thinkertoys: A Handbook of Creative-Thinking Techniques*. 2nd ed. Berkeley, Calif.: Ten Speed Press, 2006.

Millman, Debbie. *How to Think Like a Great Graphic Designer*. New York: Allworth Press, 2007.

Mollerup, Per. *Marks of Excellence: The History and Taxonomy of Trademarks*. London: Phaidon, 1999.

Mollerup, Per. *Wayshowing: A Guide to Environmental Signage Principles and Practices*. Baden: Lars Müller Publishers, 2005.

Saffer, Dan. *Designing for Interaction: Creating Innovative Applications and Devices*. 2nd ed. Berkeley, Calif.: New Riders, 2010.

Saffer, Dan. *Designing Gestural Interfaces*. Sebastopol, Calif.: O'Reilly Media, 2009.

Samara, Timothy. *Making and Breaking the Grid: A Graphic Design Layout Workshop.* Beverly, Mass.: Rockport Publishers, 2002.

Samara, Timothy. *Typography Workbook: A Real-World Guide to Using Type in Graphic Design.* Gloucester, Mass.: Rockport Publishers, 2004.

Shaughnessy, Adrian. *How to Be a Graphic Designer, Without Losing Your Soul.* New York: Princeton Architectural Press, 2005.

Shedroff, Nathan. *Design Is the Problem: The Future of Design Must Be Sustainable.* Brooklyn: Rosenfeld Media, 2009.

Sherin, Aaris. *SustainAble: A Handbook of Materials and Applications for Graphic Designers and Their Clients.* Beverly, Mass.: Rockport Publishers, 2008.

Spiekermann, Erik and E.M. Ginger. *Stop Stealing Sheep & Find Out How Type Works.* 2nd ed. Berkeley, Calif.: Adobe Press, 2003.

Sullivan, Luke. *Hey, Whipple, Squeeze This: A Guide to Creating Great Ads.* New York: John Wiley & Sons, 1998.

Visocky O'Grady, Jennifer and Ken Visocky O'Grady. *The Information Design Handbook.* Cincinnati: HOW Books, 2008.

Wheeler, Alina. *Designing Brand Identity: An Essential Guide for the Whole Branding Team.* 3rd ed. Hoboken, N.J.: John Wiley & Sons, 2009.

Yamashita, Keith and Sandra Spataro. *Unstuck.* New York: Portfolio, 2007.

Exercise Index

Permissions

23-5 ©2009 Katharine Widdows

24-1 ©2009 Jessica Thrasher

24-2 ©2009 Donnie Dinch

24-3 ©2009 Katharine Widdows

24-4 ©2009 Mark Notermann

24-5 ©2009 David Sherwin

25-1,2 ©2009 David Sherwin

25-4 ©2009 David Sherwin

25-3 ©2009 Britta Burrus Design

26-2 ©2009 Jessica Thrasher

26-1 ©2009 David Everly

26-3 ©2009 David Sherwin

27-1,2,3,4,5,6,7,8,9 ©2009 Nicholas J. Nawroth

28-4 ©2009 David Sherwin. Film images ©2009 Wes Kim

28-1,2,3 ©2009 Grace Soto

29-1,2,3,4 ©2009 Jerry Lofquist

29-5,6 ©2009 Mark Notermann

29-7 ©2009 Donnie Dinch

30-1,2,3 ©2009 Michelle Cormack

31-1,2 ©2009 Michelle Cormack

31-3 ©2009 Katharine Widdows

32-1 Design ©2009 Jake Rae. Concept ©2009 Jake Rae and Michelle Cormack

32-2 Sketch ©2009 Katharine Widdows

33-1,2,3 ©2009 Cody Moore / Waking Illustration

33-4,5 ©2009 Katharine Widdows

34-1 ©2009 Mark Notermann

34-3 ©2009 Jessica Thrasher

34-2 ©2009 Jake Rae

35-2 ©2009 Jake Rae

35-1 ©2009 Michelle Cormack

35-3 ©2009 Katharine Widdows

36-1,2,3,4,5,6 ©2009 Jarred Elrod

37-1,2,3,4 ©2009 Dave Fletcher

37-5 ©2009 Lawrence Miller

38-1,2 ©2009 Jessica Thrasher

38-3 ©2009 Jake Rae

39-1,2,3,4,5,6,7,8 ©2009 Cody Moore, Waking Illustration

40-1,2,3,4,5,6,7,8,9,10,11 ©2009 Melanie Gilliam

41-1,2,3 Design ©2009 Mark Notermann. Logo ©2009 Woodland Park Zoo

42-2,3,4 ©2009 Tom Price

42-1 ©2009 Artists for Humanity

44-1,2 ©2009 Carrie Byrne

44-3 Artwork ©2009 Ethan Martin. ©2009 Photograph by Kariann Burleson

44-1 Video ©2009 Scott Scheff and David Sherwin. Logo ©2009 Mark Notermann

45-1,2,3,4,5 ©2009 Grace Cheong

46-2,3 ©2009 Melanie Noel

47-1 ©2009 Mark Baskinger

47-2 ©2009 Jason May

48-1,2 ©2009 Claire Kohler

48-3,4 Concept ©2009 Mark Notermann and Claire Kohler. Design ©2009 Mark Notermann

49-1 Concept ©2009 Shimon Alkon. Photograph ©2009 David Sherwin

49-2 ©2009 Jake Zukowski, Abdullah Shaikh and Jeff Glasser

49-3,4,5 ©2009 David Sherwin

50-2 ©2009 Meg Doyle

50-1 ©2009 Claire Kohler

50-3 ©2009 Michelle Cormack

50-4 ©2009 Lisa Stewart, ECStewart Designs

51-1,2,3,4,5,6 ©2009 Grace Cheong

52-1,2,3,4 ©2009 Katharine Widdows. Photographs ©2009 David Sherwin

53-1,2,3 ©2009 Katharine Widdows. Source photographs ©2009 Claire Kohler

53-4 ©2009 Mark Notermann. Source photographs ©2009 Claire Kohler

53-5 ©2009 Jessica Thrasher. Source photograph ©2009 Claire Kohler

54-1,2,3 ©2009 Mark Notermann

54-4,5 ©2009 Tom Takigayama

54-6,7 ©2009 Katharine Widdows

55-1,2,3,4 ©2009 Dave Fletcher

56-1,2,3 ©2009 frog design

57-1,2 ©2009 Brian LaRossa

57-3 Photo ©2009 Jan Habraken

58-1,2,3 ©2009 Tithi Kutchamuch

58-4,5 ©2009 Katie Greff

59-1,2 ©2009 David Sherwin and Michelle Cormack

59-3,4 Design ©2009 Donnie Dinch. Concept ©2009 Donnie Dinch and Mark Notermann

59-5 ©2009 Aynex Mercado

59-6 ©2009 Meg Doyle and David Sherwin

60-1,2 ©2009 Donnie Dinch

60-3 ©2009 Meg Doyle and Mark Notermann

Check out these other great books and offers from HOW Books!

  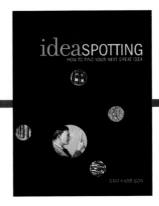

In *Creative Grab Bag*, author Ethan Bodnar asked a variety of artists to take on a task outside the realm of their normal work. Each task—for instance, designing a building, illustrating a memory, designing an album cover—was randomly selected from a grab bag he created. The result is a collection of work brimming with creative energy. Tear-out cards are also included so you can do the creative challenges yourself.

#Z2388, 224 pages, paperback, ISBN: 978-1-60061-147-6

Chock-full of useful 15-minute exercises designed to help creative types tap into their daily creative buzz, *Caffeine for the Creative Mind* is perfect for limbering up your imagination on a daily basis. With simple and conceptual exercises, this guide will have you reaching for markers, pencils, digital cameras and more in order to develop a working and productive creative mindset.

#Z0164, 360 pages, paperback, ISBN: 978-1-58180-867-4

In this book, seasoned business pro Sam Harrison offers real and unique insight into the creative process, as well as exercises to help anyone generate viable business ideas. *IdeaSpotting* trains business people and creative people alike to step outside of their daily routine to find that next great idea by encouraging spontaneity and exploration.

#33478, 256 pages, paperback, ISBN: 978-1-58180-800-1

➡ **Find these books and many others at MyDesignShop.com or your local bookstore.**

SPECIAL OFFER

You can get 15% off your *entire order* at MyDesignShop.com! All you have to do is go to http://www.howdesign.com/cwoffer and sign up for our free e-newsletter on graphic design. You'll also get a free digital download of the latest issue of HOW magazine.